Musings of the Day; Vol. 1

By Kathy LaFollett

Cover Art – James Gannon
Cover Design – Kathy LaFollett

ISBN - 9781549918896

Musings began May 11th, 2016 on my personal Facebook page. Intended as simple writing exercises, they fast became open windows and doors to what came and went in my day. You might call this a diary, but that wouldn't define musings properly. You might consider this a "note to self" as well. But that too, would fall short of what started in May of 2016.

Musings are a still frame to the truth of my daily life. The truth is our shared truth. We are so much more alike than we are different. The truth is my days aren't more important or impressive than any other's day becomes. We all have our preferred building blocks to create our lifestyle.

The truth is our days are magical and full of sparks of light and laughter. Our lives are our personal sparkler and we should run through time with it firing off sparks of inspiration to everyone who takes the time to look. We are all a light that was meant to be shared.

2016

5-11-16
Piggles are guinea pigs. You'll need to remember that for this book.

A bunny blowing his coat looks like a bison on the open range. Swaths of long fur hanging, falling, leaving behind short perfectly mowed fur. A bunny can eat like a bison, too.

Two month old piggles will learn to identify the sound of a refrigerator door in 3 days.

14 year old dogs with dementia and powerful noses will eat anything that comes close to smelling like food. And afterward forget they ate it.

Blue and Gold Macaws will steal every hair twisty you put in your hair. ALL. DAY. LONG. Buy economy sized packages of hair twisties. And stock shares in a hair accessory company. You might just break even.

When your French coffee press is empty of all your Cafe Du Monde coffee, this is sad. Buy a bigger French press. Don't be sad.

Felix sits quietly on his digesting perch after breakfast IF his apple chunks were laid on top of his carrot shavings. Otherwise, dementia dog will have a meal of upside down carrots and apples and not remember a thing.

It's only 10:44 in the morning. I've learned so much before lunch.

5-13-16
Felix is our African Grey Parrot. Jamal-Pierre is his guinea pig.
I am Felix's Trainee.

A 1200 gram piggles will teach a 452 gram African Grey to talk like a piggles. Thanks Jamal-Pierre. Felix's "veep" is a ton of fun. The first 100 times.

A bunny, once introduced into his playroom, will not leave his playroom willingly. And by willingly I mean without kicking me in the face.

Buy more hair twisties.

A Horde of Cockatiels will let you know when the mailman walks by the window. And by let you know I mean flapping wings like possessed bats while blowing all the foraging contents out of their flight cage and onto the floor. Thank you mailman.

Turtles wondering in the backyard looking for the lake across the street are really black-hearted macaw assassins of death. Butters told me so after I peeled her off the ceiling.

A Kirby is an Indian Ringneck Parakeet. And a force to be acknowledged.
The Horde is a 4 member flock of cockatiels that follow a Kirby's lead.

Kirby Lurker must lurk. And buzz. And steal food from all food bowls. And squeeze through openings the size of an atom to get into spaces the size of a postage stamp to look for food he may have missed. Which leaves me looking inside Kirby sized openings to find spaces the size of a Kirby to find my Lurker. I didn't need that hour and half anyway.

Doing laundry and finishing laundry is simply the difference between having a sleeping macaw or a fully aware macaw. I suggest the former if you don't have clean underpants.

No, no I didn't want any of that popcorn in that bowl I just set down Horde Members. I'm sure the dogs will enjoy all that I didn't pop for them.

Crab dip isn't real crab dip until your parrot has walked through it.

A sleepy bunny isn't really asleep. They are a version of trapdoor spider waiting for the next sucker to open the door and look in. I didn't need THAT 45 minutes either.

5-17-16

The devil's in the details. Werthers is my other guinea pig.
That's a detail you should remember.

When feeding companions it's important to remember Felix does not want vegetables or fruits in his top bowl, only the interior bowl, unless dad is home. Those bowls then become irrelevant.

Snickers and Butters require the exact same content of all bowls dry and fresh except Snickers fresh bowl that must have 3 raspberries not 1. Butters fresh bowl must have 1 raspberry that she won't eat.

Kirby requires one bowl with a bit of something from every other bowl in the house but, won't eat any of that anyway. Because Kirby's cage is an insult to Kirby. Snickers will eat from that, but only after Butters clears the stuff Snickers won't touch.

The Horde must have their mix presented in pie formation with fresh herbs against pellets, and a slice of cut green beans and snap peas. Not too big, or small or they'll just toss it on the floor for dogs. This is how you get dogs to eat their vegetables.

Werthers wants his alfalfa hay next to his botanical hay with a sprinkling of timothy hay first cuts on top. Unless the alfalfa hay has more top flowers. Then screw all that and just dump alfalfa to right of the water bottle, because that water bottle is ridiculous and below his standards. You can't soak hay in a water bottle. Green bits better be leafy because he isn't eating anything that isn't leafy and light. Jamal-Pierre prefers his timothy hay stacked outside of the hay box. In fact, why IS that hay box in there anyway? Because PetSmart's profit line isn't fat enough, that's why. And I take moving the economy seriously.

Jamal-Pierre enjoys botanical hay, timothy hay, orchard grass and first cut organic alfalfa hay hidden at the bottom for a surprise. Which leads to all
other hay being thrown out the top of his corral and onto Turner. Who now looks like a tumble weed. Who knew yorkies could tumble so well.

Leopard Geckos have teeth. Sharp little pokey teeth. I know this because my geckos are 7 inches long with mouths 1 inch wide and require being fed by hand. And they are farsighted.

A Bun with a strawberry top has no interest in much else. Except another strawberry top.

Somewhere in this house is my coffee I set down 30 minutes ago.

5-18-16
Snickers is our male scarlet macaw. I make a point to point that out because the boys are a handful. In fact, Snickers' nickname is TwoHandsFull.

Salmon Spread tastes better with a Lurker on your shoulder. I don't know why, but it does. Wait, I know why. Because everything is better with a parrot on your shoulder. That's why.

If Snickers wants to sing "Snickers you're a good boy howudoin?" for three hours straight, I will always keep a front row seat.

Bunnies like paper towel rolls. They also like you to throw them back after they pitch one to you. Forget that last part and you face an insulted bunny. Just throw the thing.

Be careful what you wish for...wait. Don't do that. Make some seriously disco wishes and sit back and enjoy the show.

Today is a wonderful day. It is because there is only one of them. It's precious like a diamond, or a good friend, or a loving spouse...or a parrot. Or a piggles, or a giggle or a bunny, or your amazing children or really just about any little or big thing. Your life is not a dress rehearsal. It is a one time only carnival game. Go play fearlessly.

There are raspberry bird feet tracks on the floor. This seems reasonable to me.

5-23-16

No matter what you do to a Smoothie Blend, adding Organic Apple Cider Vinegar makes it taste not smooth.

A bunny is part mountain goat and bull in a china shop. I shall name this new species Leonidas BunBullGoat. There is no BunBullGoat-proofing known to man.

Seriously Butters I'm getting my hair cut short and you can hang off the back of no hair at all and like it!

BunBullGoat 9 - Mom 0. I need a Fitbit bracelet to track my step count running up and down stairs to fix all my useless BunBullGoat proofing ideas. I'm pretty sure I'm at 10,000 steps now. I think I hear Leo laughing up there. Creating a Bun Playroom on the second floor is cardio.

When an African Grey says, "See the Birdie" this does not mean he wants you to come over and look at him.

Old dogs are like thunder. You can tell their age by how long it takes them to react to things. Bruiser waited 14 minutes to bark at the mailman that was no longer there. His heart was in it though. Okay not really, he just sat up and barked a while and looked at me like he forgot why he got up for something 14 minutes ago. This works for humans as well.

5-27-16

A bunny's ears change shape depending on their mood. Like a mood ring, but furry. And long. And there are two of them.

It is easier to drink coffee when there is not a small bird perched on the handle of your coffee mug. Write that down.

Butters is happy I can still wear hair twisties. Butters is surprised how easy they are to pull out now that my hair is shorter. Stock Tip of the Day; buy Target shares. I'm about to double my purchases over there.

A small piggles falls asleep anywhere. A large piggles boops your face to remind you to sit still so he can fall asleep.

An African Grey who believes the bird room is for birds will be insulted to find a bunny running in circles in said room. Also, a parrot yelling "BAD BIRD!" at a bunny is hilarious.

A Lurker on the side of your popcorn bowl will throw out more than he eats, less than you try to protect, and about the same as falls on the floor. I think I heard a dog burp.

When Felix asks for popcorn, he wants popcorn, warm tea, moved next to the computer so I can dole out popcorn he isn't going to eat anyway because he really only wanted to be next to me, and one raisin. Do NOT forget the raisin.

When every word you type, every word you speak and every effort you make is sincerely sincere, and offered with hopes of helping, insincerity in return rather hurts. More than I want to sincerely admit.

A Scarlet Macaw sincerely bumping your leg with a big yellowy-white and black beak while tugging on your shirt with a big clunky foot for a head scratch, is so very sincere it becomes humbling. I totally forgot what I was thinking about.

6-2-16

The more successful you are creating trust and joy with your companions, the less you will be able to eat, sleep, clean, drink, walk, sit, lay, crawl, hide, talk, shower, pee, computer, phone, laundry, dishes or think alone. Success carefully people.

The garbage truck just rumbled past the house. I am offering comfort to two macaws, one grey and one IRN while typing with one hand and two fingers. There's a math equation in there somewhere.

Currently Kirby is executing speed laps around the house. He should win pole position from the sounds of the WHOOSH! behind me.

A rabbit can train a Horde of Cockatiels given enough time.

Snickers likes the front window blind up. Felix wants it down. Butters doesn't care if she's left alone on my right shoulder, Kirby is too busy on lap 73 to notice but I'm pretty sure he appreciates the extra light at the apex of his turn, and the garbage truck is a block away. This all should get interesting in a few minutes.

6-7-16

No matter how well I clean my ears I still so appreciate the Butters Mobile Ear Cleaning Service.

When sharing a fresh vegetable and fruit blend with a Lurker, wear rain gear.

Once a piggles realizes they can control you with their Veep Powers there is no going back. Pretending it's not happening, or denying you are carrying around a piggles for 20 minutes because you are now a Piggles Cruise Ship, is futile.

A bored macaw will out think any human in the room. Like a super computer, but with feathers and intent.

I've started making my coffee before rather than after 19 bowls and 4 water bottles. Thank you me. That all went much smoother.

Tropical Storm Colin released the frogs. Currently our backyard is louder than our macaws. Which makes me smile a little bigger.

We lost our little dog, Turner, Friday. He left our backyard it seems. It is so very hard waiting for some sign, a call, or an email to come and make things easy again. He is so small and light, but his empty space is so huge and heavy. Every corner I turn in our neighborhood I imagine him there. Every glance outside I imagine him there. Every thought on an idea brings him into my mind.

Life goes on, no matter the weight we carry. Be kind. Your kindness in a short moment may be the only time and place another person can set their weight down to rest.

6-19-16

I am now on double super secret probation by Kirby. Since coming back home from my speaking engagement he has not let me leave his sight nor has he left my shoulder. I can no longer be trusted. I have broken the Kirby Circle of Trust.

Having shared Gate A6 for 7 hours with a few hundred of my fellow human flyers due to weather delays, I can honestly say we are all, collectively and individually, odd.

Butters' talons are so sharp right now she could take up parrot needlepoint.

Coffee at home is still better than coffee in the best of hotels. And that was a really nice hotel.

Getting one's head on straight after letting it swivel freely for three days is tricky business. I may need a couple days to reboot.

6-24-16

A plumber walked into our kitchen/dining yesterday and found one bunny, one piggles, one African Grey, two dogs and four cockatiels. He asked how many kids we had. "Nine in this room." I answered.

Coffee. Is. So. Perfect. With half-n-half. Not milk. No sugar either. Other than that, perfect.

Turner lost 20% of his body weight while he was out lost in the big bad world. He lost 0% of his Yorky Attitude. Bruiser is currently deciding whether or not he is happy about Turner's return.

I get to write all day today. All. Day. This is a good thing.

Felix is running for President of the United States. After the most excellent people of Britain seized the day, I see this is as perfectly normal.

A macaw can fall in love with toe nail clippers. Be advised.

When bringing a bunny home you are also installing a full Home Monitoring and Motion Detecting Surveillance System. If an intruder tries to break in, your dog tries to walk down stairs, you try to go to the bathroom, or a cricket wakes up your Motion Detecting Bunny with immediately THUMP THUMP while throwing his blocks across his condo while running up the ramp to the second floor to THUMP louder while tossing his paper cups down to the condo's first floor. This will trigger the Secondary Warning Terrier System to immediately roll over and start licking your face. After that, it's up to you to handle your defenses.

7-1-16

If a bunny is excited to see you, you have passed the test of Nice Human. If a piggles is excited to see you, you have passed the test of Good Waiter. If a dog is excited to see you, he needs to go out. If a parrot is excited to see you, you have passed the Excellent Human Test; relax and enjoy the endorsements.

The number of holes chewed in your shirt is a direct reflection of how much you are loved. By your companion parrot. If you don't have a parrot, you should probably go clothes shopping.

There is a Big Blue Chicken in her bedroom cage one foot up right now. Obviously somebody isn't ready to wake up. Snickers is patiently waiting on top of Butters' cage. And by patiently I mean flying around, landing, hanging upside down and yelling "SNICKERdoodles!" through Butters' bedroom cage door.

You know you are smack dab in the middle of a good life when a 3 day weekend presents itself, and it's no different to you than the last weekend.

I was so stressed out worrying about things yesterday, I had to read my own musings to calm down. That was weird.

7-4-16

This was a long 4th weekend around here. Drunken neighbors shouting for hours on end, fireworks randomly invading space and time, cars traveling too fast, and screams carrying on too late into the night. Our 3 day experiences gave me pause personally. I want to apologize publicly.

I am so very sorry to all the neighbors I selfishly affected long ago. For years I shot fireworks off with friends in backyards during the 4th. I paid no attention to the time nor place. There were no laws forcing me to take that moment of consideration. I am sorry to those who suffered the environmental pollutions I selfishly put into our lawns and environment. I carelessly released heavy metals, sulfur, carbons and noxious gases for hours. I apologize.

I apologize for the random decibel abuse I released into your personal space. I had no right. And yet with selfish, and sometimes drunken verve I invaded the personal spaces of dozens of neighbors, again, for hours on end. I am so very sorry to those who were anxious, those struggling with PTSD, and those who are sensitive to those abusive, loud sounds that are meant to mimic cannon fire and bombs. I brought the sound of war to your home and I had no right. I am so sorry.

I am sorry for tormenting the wildlife with those pollutants and terrifying warfare sounds and flashes of light. At dusk we would start, after the songbirds long roosted. And we continued until we ran out of armaments. What fear and distress I conjured all those times. What hours of terror did I add up for an innocent population that I claimed to love and appreciate. I am ashamed knowing my selfish impact.

I am sorry for tormenting my neighbors companions. Dogs, cats, parrots and the like. I had no right to inflict that unnecessary stress on those that you love and protect. I am so very sorry for my selfish acts.

Fireworks are meant to do one thing, and ask any historian who understands the birth of these chemical bombs in China. They are meant to strike fear into hearts. They are meant to replicate war in sound, smell and light. They require heavy metals, petroleum, explosive powders and sulfur to yield their affects. And like the accumulated amounts of Lead at firing ranges, heavy metal fall out results during firework displays large and small. We literally pollute the ground and air. We literally pollute with sound and light as well. We bring war to our neighbors, wildlife and companions when no one would voluntarily ask for same.

We take chances of fire, injury and death with these products. Every year homes are lit afire, people loose body parts, and children are burned to emulate war. I took those chances all those years. I want to apologize to my neighbors for putting their property at risk. I want to apologize to friends who I may have come so very close in harming.

Yes, this long 3 day war and drinking theatre brought the reality of my past selfishness. And yes I am so very sorry for those times. Because, if I impacted people around me as much as those around us affected our family this past weekend, I just feel like a jerk. A selfish, thoughtless, mindless, arrogant jerk. And I am sorry.

7-6-16

There's something comforting and familiar in the sound of a neighbor mowing their lawn.

There's a preening macaw on my head. There's also a lovely cascade of white fluff feathers and feather casings drifting downward in front of my face. It's like a snowy Christmas morn. If a snowy Christmas morn includes 2 pounds of macaw on your head.

Felix is one foot up on his tent that's parked to my right. He's trying to fall asleep, but I keep trying to catch him falling asleep. So he can't fall asleep because he refuses to let me catch him.

There's a piggles 15 feet away giving me the hairy eye over the top railing of his piggles condo. This could mean I failed with the morning breakfast greens. I failed with the timothy/orchard hay. I failed with the pellet ratio, or I failed to scratch his nose long enough. Whatever the cause, by the looks of him, I'm in big piggles trouble.

7-26-16

Snickers autocorrect;
"Stop. Just Stop. No you stop. Snickerdoodle is a good boy! STOP."

I've just been scolded by a bunny. I wouldn't call it demoralizing per se, just unnerving.

I'd like to think I share lunch with the flock. But I'm pretty sure I'm just handing over the loot in the end.

Although two macaws can fit on one human head, I do not recommend it.

7-29-16

I type with my right hand only. On my left sits Snickers, proudly perched on my upturned wrist. My elbow is bent at 90 degrees so he is at just the right height to look out the window in front of him. The blood supply is slowing at my elbow and ending at my wrist, due to 2 pounds of bird with a ninja grip.

I write on.

A small throbbing pulse in the bend of my elbow tells me I may want to change the position of my arm. Said attempt allows Snickers to tell me that ain't happen'n.

I write on.

Snickers donks my wrist admonishing me to stop it. It being the heavy pulse of blood fighting to reach my hand and fingers.

I write on.

Butters lands on my right shoulder and succinctly pulls the hair twisty from my pony tailed hair for her personal amusement. I don't really notice due the heavy tingle in my left hand now.

I write on.

I hear Kirby fly around the corner at the same time Butters drops the hair twisty she really didn't want. All the while I think, yes...yes I do believe my hand could fall off from the lack of an oxygenated blood supply. Kirby lands vertical on the back of my T-shirt hanging like a little blue bat.

I write on.

Butters takes exception and chases Kirby off by sliding down my back via her hooked beak on my T-shirt collar which chokes my airway temporarily while forcing me to lower my arm to save my life to make sure Butters doesn't fall to the floor. Kirby flew off long before her first move. You can't catch a Lurker so easily. Snickers releases my dead arm and flys off with his signature call of insult. I'm pretty sure it's a curse word if translated from parrot speak.

I write on with one hand. And a numb and tingly left arm hanging at my side. And Felix proclaiming calmly, "It's allll RIGHT!"

8-4-16

Butters, formally known as a Blue and Gold Macaw, can now be referred to as 2.1 pounds of Blue and Gold Velcro.

Snickers is either guarding my desk from villains who may enter through the front door, holding a yoga pose through breath, or waiting for me not to see him trying to chew on my desk. I'll let you know in a minute how that worked out.

Jamal-Pierre and Werthers are currently veeping to each other, pining for their play time. Sure I'll put them together for their play time. It's all fun and games until one of them decides their penis is bigger than the others and it's a teeth chatter - boxes knocking over - rattling water bottles - hay slinging bar fight. Then it's back to pining in their own homes. The boys need their two story hutch if they are going to live together. It's like HGTV meets eHarmony without all the questions or decorating tips.

It's raining hard. The local Muscovy ducks are under our magnolia tree waiting and watching. I. Love. Ducks.

Kirby is upstairs in the master bath, perched on the hand towel ring buzzing like a ham radio. A ham radio Kirby is a very happy Kirby.

8-8-16

I have a back-scratcher. It is awesome. It is not a parrot. It is bamboo. It is also a thing of hellish fear inducing threat to all the birds. I'm waiting for Snickers to grab it, drop it, scream at it and dismantle it. He's a Hellish Fear Inducing Threat Assassin.

LeoBun will let me brush his butt if he's eating a baby carrot. Every one has a price.

It's a dark and rainy day. The Horde line up in a close knit row on dark and rainy days as they look out the dark and wet window. They are so cute alloopreening each other right now. Watching them be so happy in such a simple way reminds me to calm down and appreciate the little things. Like the 2.1 pound Blue and Gold Velcro parrot on my head.

It's raining, and has been for a while now. The neighbor is mowing in the rain with a lawn mower that does not want to mow wet grass. And quite frankly from the sound of it's dismay I'm betting that mower isn't impressed with dry grass either. Have mercy on that mower, neighbor. Seriously. Let it go man.

8-11-16

Grumpy LeoBun ran up the ramp to his second story nap area. He's about over the flock calling among the parrots. Currently he's looking out the wired door window all grumpy grandpa thumping. His first Thump of Disdain was simple enough. Just a light tap of "Knock it off!"

Kirby and The Horde continue their Glorious Morning calls anyway.

His second through 12th thumps progressing into Bunny Ear Shakes of Doom Thumps. Heavy Jumpn'Thumps of Irritation if you will.

Felix joins Kirby and The Horde mimicking the Horde's own Glorious Morning Calls anyway.

LeoBun's 13th through 19th thumps progress into Bunny Ear Shakes with Triple Lindy BunQuake Thumps. Followed by Echoing OlympicBun Thumps of RAWR!

At this rate Leo may just blow another coat in there.

Snickers and Butters just flew into the scene adding Glorious Dactyl Jungle Screams of Joy.

Final Score:
Parrots 3 - Grumpy Grandpa LeoBun 0

8-15-16

Felix is not impressed with my Parrot Party Convention Hats. As a Presidential Candidate he's rather difficult really. We're on take 7 for our Parrot Party Convention Commercial and all I'm getting out of this Candidate is; "Awwwwwww!" like some old grumpy guy dismissing an annoying 7 year old child.

No one votes for the old grumpy guys!

For the record I am not an annoying 7 year old child either. Neener.

I've run out of blueberries and sweet peppers. I can not be sure, but I believe there is a Piggles Coup being planned.

Seriously, if no one hears from me, send help. I'll be barricaded in the upstairs closet.

I'm not a killer. I prefer to allow and promote nature to do her thing. I do not look at rats or mice as evil. They have a reason to be here. They are nature's buffet for owls, hawks, snakes and such. So when we moved into our new home in 1999 and found a rat living comfortably under our raised deck, I shrugged that little fellow off.

"More power to you my friend." I whispered with a tip o'the hat. "I just saw two, 4 foot black racer snakes. Good luck with all that."

Our local wildlife snakes did their job for quite some time.

Until they didn't.

2016 and I've learned an interesting human tendency. We humans do not like riots or large groups assembling. Particularly under our raised decks. It changes beliefs and perspective on murder.

I'm still not a killer. But I am not a Holiday Inn for a small group of rodentia representing 3 generations of hangers on!

Where are my snakes!?! Losers. Slackers. Carpetbaggers! LIARS!

Here's the flip to my flipping out. I do not mind murdering palmetto bugs at will. *Do not google that bug to see an image. No good can come from gazing upon it's hellish face.*

Okay. Wait. I do mind murdering them to a degree because it requires;
A) I look at them.
B) I touch them (the sole of my shoe counts) and
C) I have to look at them again to clean up the carnage left behind by my shoe.

BUT, I do not mind killing them in massive numbers if I'm not wearing my glasses. I kid you not I will take my glasses off to murder palmettos. At that point they just look like blurry brown blobs. I can compartmentalize myself through that idea.

All that being said, since our Holiday Inn residencies got into the second and third generation I haven't seen one damnable palmetto.

So I asked myself, are these rodentia of 3 generations eating said beasties from the pit of Hades? Because the timeline supports a circle of life thing here.

I am today, sitting in the middle of two truths. It's time for an eviction process to begin. But alas, that will eventually welcome back Satan's Spawn into the place vacated by said current residents.

I ponder this issue, applying a 5 star reviewed organic and green product called Critter Out between the boards of the raised deck. I can hear the squeaks and scrambling of said residents under eviction. I also pondered the fact that the Zika Virus is now in my County.

So you see, I may have bigger fish to fry. Like mosquitoes.

On a side note; The parrots are fabulously happy watching me through the window while I scream and jump as the crickets come up from between the deck boards like a horde of chirping lava while I spray.

In all my trials and tribulations, I always aim to entertain.

8-24-16

Butters perched at the highest point of the biggest tree stand puts her at about 6 feet up, maybe 6.6. At any rate she's looking down at me as if I've asked the epoch of stupid questions. Why should she get down? Why should she step up? Why should she do anything being the super powered parrot in the room? I'll vacuum around and under her since she's winning this Q & A session.

LeoBun's condo is cleaned, updated and filled with new Dixie cups, bedding, paper towel rolls, one freshly washed stuffed bear and 2 pristine sheets of paper towels. All placed carefully IN THE WRONG PLACES. LeoBun is not amused. But he's busy!

I won the battle of the rat residency today. I watched a number of them run off while I was applying the repellent yesterday and have not seen whisker nor hair of them in their usual daily runs and stances today. I did a follow-up application for good measure and slight attitude adjustment. A little tip for using Critter Out; Apply 10 times the application recommendation. Yesterday I used about 3000 sq. ft. of product coverage on 400 sq. ft. The squirrels won't even come up by the deck now and are slightly more than put off with my arrogance. I'm pretty sure one flipped me off earlier.

I'm enrolling Werthers into the Julliard School of Drama. Opening the refrigerator sends him into the death scene from some Shakespearean tragedy. I'm not sure if he wants lettuce or if he's dying of a sword inflicted wound on a battlefield in France. I swear he grabbed his chest and fell backwards when I looked at him.

8-26-16

I had lunch with my husband today at Sab Cafe. I have to tell you that to tell you the rest of this. I LOVE Sab's Pho. It's just too perfect.

I add that Chili Sauce that's in the squeeze bottle on the table. Just enough to turn the broth from a golden color to a deep umber. Then I squeeze both the lime wedges into it, add the mint, and a bit of everything off the greens plate. It's so hot, it's so good. I'm so greedy with my chopsticks, they can barely hold the amount of noodles I want to shovel in my face. Seriously this is the one food that declares I have the ability to be a foodie.

I always bring home about half as it's a massive serving. So here I am, back at home, trying to get my wheels under me while suffering food coma. A couple hours pass and I'm ready to finish my Pho, with a beer and a Felix. Because really, what's the point of wheels at 3:30 in the afternoon on a Friday.

Felix has never tried my Pho before and for whatever reason he's all about what I have in this steaming bowl, and those chop sticks are interesting, too.

I have learned Pho turns African Grey Parrots into ravenous, demanding Vikings. Pho also brings out new words and sounds. Probably memories from his days as a Viking.

He's making slurping sounds I've never heard before. He's mumbling something about something and "Mmmm" and "that's good, huh?" I turn away from serving him to take a mouthful of rice noodles while there's still some left and just as the chopsticks are at my mouth...

"HERE! Here! that's good, huh? HERE!" Ravenous. Demanding. Viking.

He's so full he didn't bother demanding to go back to his digesting perch. He just turned around, away from his now empty bowl on his tent and knocked off.

Which is really a great idea. But Kirby's howling for mercy and freedom sounds like I may not get to follow Felix's lead.

9-6-16

Notes on team work, or lack thereof.

He lays there stretched out in the corner watching my handy work. His nose twitches and he licks his bunny lips as if to say, "Continue, peasant". I work my way toward him clearing bedding, shredded Dixie cups, coco-bunny-puff poo and the errant wood piece chewed from the condo itself. The closer I get to LeoBun, the less his nose twitches. I've cleaning to do and a focus only a peasant can possess. I spot a nice wad of bedding with embedded LeoBun fur, hay twigs and Dixie cup shreds half covered by LeoBun's own belly. He lays there lightly breathing. Waiting. Although invoking dread I want to kiss that Bun nose. I move slightly closer with an eye for that nice wad. I want it. I want it in the garbage. LeoBun stretches and yawns. I think this is an invitation to remove the nice wad.

I am sorely mistaken.

Blinded by pelting Dixie cups hitting my head I realize LeoBun took his nice wad and ran up the ramp to the second floor before the cups settled. He looks out the second story door at me with a certainty I won't soon forget. You've won this time Leonidas. THIS time.

A Kirby does not need a cage. A Kirby needs a human to wear cotton T-shirts that accommodate Kirby talons. You only think Velcro is impressive until you've tried removing a Kirby Lurker from your T-shirt.

13 year old Yorkshire Terriers can tap dance. I know this because Turner puts on a floor show every night at 5:00 pm. He's fed at 5:30 pm. There's no disconnect there.

Our new washer has a myriad of tones and playlists. It sounds a lovely tune every time a cycle is done. It sounds another lovely tune when you are choosing cycles and settings. Felix is practicing these tonal tunes. Kirby is working with him. Nothing good can come from this.

9-8-16

Felix never leaves his cage or tree stand area without Taxi Service. He rarely gets on the floor, and only flys if Dad's proximity requires it.

Until he doesn't.

I'm busy practicing my speech for the Long Island Parrot EXPO and realize after the end of the second run-through and two hours of not paying attention that Felix isn't anywhere. I call out, "Felix!"

He calls back, "See the birdie?"

19

Lord have mercy. We have hardwood floors and open concept and very few things hanging off the walls. I paint murals because parrots can't pull down a mural. Our house echoes like a cavern in Kentucky.

I call out again, "FELIX!"

"See the birdie?" He voice bounces and mocks me with angles of lies. I think he's over there by the couch. Nope. "Felix!!"

"See the birdie?" Under the table? Nope. Behind his tree stand? Nope. Under Jamal-Pierre behind his RV? Uh...no.

"Felix. Come on man!"

"See the birdie?" The sound moved! I think. No, I think he really traveled again. Snickers is in his cage calling...I think he's trying to tell me where Felix is...or he just hates the lawn crew behind the house.

"FELIX!" I go into the dining room.

Bruiser is dead asleep. That's how he sleeps now being so old. Like the dead. I can de-bone a cooked chicken and that dog won't wake up. Turner is asleep, also dead.

"FELIX!!"

"KirbyKIRRRBY!! Goodboy Kirbykirby!" Wrong Bird. He's in the sink anyway trying to get the last of the peanut butter off a knife.

"Fee! Dude! Where are you?"

"See the Birdie?" Seriously. I can't find this bird! I walk back into the bird room and watch the lawn guy mow the field behind our house. It's a flood plain so it obviously recovered from the storm. I get lost in that thought for a minute. Snickers is still not impressed with the mower and Butters is still on my shoulder as she has been through this whole game of Hide-n-Seek. She pulls off my hair twistie and my thinking back to finding Felix. WHERE is my bird!?

fartsound

He's at my feet. Translated fartsound means "TAG! You're it."

9-14-16
I colored my hair blue and purple about this time. I had my hair cut short and colored in all the colors of Snickers and Butters blue and purple. Mostly because I thought it would be easier for people to spot me in crowds during the EXPO. I was right about that.

Blue Hair Report:

Felix doesn't care.

Kirby doesn't care.

Snickers cared for a couple of hours and tried to remove said blue hair from my head. Realized during hour 3, it's just me in blue hair. Snickers doesn't care, now.

Butters thinks the blue hair is not me and does not belong and can not be trusted and therefore must be shunned. She's currently fighting two truths unsuccessfully. Blue Hair is evil. Must have hair twisty holding short blue hair. Poor Butters.

Werthers likes popcorn. I know this because I sat down by his cage to watch a bit of Werthers TV and eat popcorn. The regularly scheduled programming was interrupted by my popcorn and Werthers' nose meeting for the first time. I let him take a sniff of a fluffy kernel. I guess he thought I meant eat it because he hung out and reached through the cage bars like a crazed zombie trying to get to fresh non-zombies for dinner. Werthers really likes popcorn.

9-26-16

Butters had a grooming session at her vet's. She pout-growled all the way there, goose-honked all the way through, and said Snickers name over and over and over all the way home. I'm sure there's a macaw code in all of that.

Felix has replaced his favorite of pistachios with Sriracha cashews. I know. I had to sit down for for that one myself.

Thunder not only sets off car alarms, but piggles as well.

There's a FABULOUS male African Grey available for adoption at our vet's office. His name is Scoley. Imagine my inner argument. Go ahead...imagine that conversation.

Today was Dad's first day back at work after being on vacation for 11 days and gone for 7 of those. Currently not one bird believes he's coming home from work. And one bird is more interested in Sriracha cashews than whether or not they are right about that.

9-28-16

Butters does not like otters. Specifically Butters does not like otters;

a) rubbing their butts on her fence.

b) wrestling by her fence.
c) wrestling and rubbing their butts by and on her fence.

Otters do not care.

Additionally Butters' Otter Alarm sounds quite a bit like her Turtle Alarm.

LeoBun does not like Butters' alarms.

Butters does not care.

Otters do not like white egrets walking over and interrupting their fence grooming. Their Egret Alarm sounds like a cross between a chihuahua and a harbor seal.

Egret does not care.

It seems to me it'd be a lot quieter around here if every body would be a bit more considerate.

10-7-16

Snickers broke the tip of his beak yesterday. It's not off yet, just a little 1/8th inch piece askew and hanging there, the break goes across not up. That all being said. Ouchy! I spoon fed him rice and chicken last night with a little spoon to the side of his beak. He ate fresh orange slices.

Today he's gingerly traveling and I realized the tip is still there. So it's going to be an uncomfortable couple days for him. I chopped soft fruits into proper chunks, and put them in a bowl with filter water/fresh squeezed orange juice to float in, and big chunky pellets to soak up the water/juice. I hand fed him breakfast from this bowl.

Mom is sMothering. sMothering is one of my talents.

And then Dactyl Mode kicked in.

Butters confiscated the soft foods bowl like a pirate. Snickers went to the window bowl with normal dry foods and I was like, "NO! Butters! Snickers is injured and crippled and incapable of eating anything but that from the sMothering Menu!!!"

Or not.

He's just eating sideways. And on my head right now.

When I had human kids I could force them to lay on a couch with a bendy straw and 7-Up. And they stayed there.

Snickers' beak is all better. He figured this out yesterday around 3:30 pm when it was time to try and steal Felix's Foods Bowls.

Pumpkin Nuts and Spice Birdie Biscuits have made it to the top of the MUTE BUTTON treat list. You know it's on the MUTE BUTTON treat list when every bird has their own, and does not care if the other guy has one, too. Thank you for the surprise treats for feets Christine's Chop Shop. H U G E hit!!

LeoBun has learned a new game. Guilt the Mom. Basically you stand on your big back bun feet and stick your fuzzy front feet through the cage door openings while at the same time sticking an adorable twitchy bunny nose out. Flop your ears. Twitch the nose. Lick the bunny lips. THUMP.

LeoBun 31 - Mom 0.

Kirby has spent the last 15 minutes combing my hair with his beak. I haven't checked yet, but I bet I look fabulous.

Boy piggles are challenging. They want to be friends. They need to be friends, but they have to murder each other for a spot on a towel. There's a moral drenched story in there somewhere.

We've had them in separate cages in separate rooms listening, smelling and experiencing each other from afar. I would take them upstairs to the Bun Playroom for group therapy sessions. BUT they have to murder each other for a spot on the same towel.

When I came back from New York I set up Werther's cage next to Jamal-Pierre's so they could visit and talk. That was a week ago. So they chattered, thumped, grumbled, rumbled and discussed murdering each other over the same towel for a week.

Day before yesterday I noticed they both were laying next to each other separated by their cage bars. No teeth chattering, just rumbles. They must have moved off the subject of murder.

Right now they are sharing Jamal-Pierre's cage. I put all of Werthers' stuff in Jamal's cage, and took all of Jamal's into Werthers' cage for later tonight. I'm not convinced they are mature enough to sleep together unattended yet.

I'll scramble their territorial eggs instead.

Snickers, on my head, has begun the first act of "I, Parrot". An opera he wrote telling the story of his people. His performance showcases the strength of his vocabulary expressed through his amazing vocal skills. "Snickers IS a good boy!" Tells us all we need to know about the Scarlet Macaw in the wild.

It's October and mini pumpkins are available in the produce section. I buy these for the dactyls to destroy. After cleaning LeoBun's condo and replacing his Dixie Cups, paper towel rolls, paper towel sheets and grass knots with new ones, I gave him the smallest of the pumpkins. This Bun gets so excited with new things. After kicking it around, biting it, and kicking it around some more he made a napping spot with his clean bedding. Duly note; Buns like napping with mini pumpkins.

Kirby Lurker is perched on top of the Horde's Aviary. He and Stella are having some sort of dispute about something very critical to both of them. I've noticed just about everything is critical to a cockatiel. I have money on Stella winning this argument.

10-14-16

In the final chapter of transitioning two piggles for Casa de Jamal-Pierre y Werthers I cleaned out Jamal's CC Cage, put in a thick layer of carefree bedding mixed with some timothy hay, put in Werther's pellet bowl, water bowl and box, then rearranged everything to create 3 water/food stations with 2 boxes for individual napping.

I went errand running for 2 hours.

I come home to piggles napping together in one box.

I am now on my second Michelob Ultra and 6th King's Hawaiian Roll with fresh cherry tomatoes. The weekend just got real. Seriously, this is about as crazy as I get with food and weekends.

For those concerned about the low blood sugars; Felix is on his tent to my right with a bowl of pistachios and a chunk of King's Hawaiian Roll.

All others are in their cages in food comas and toy exhaustion. Because every cage becomes Toys r Us if I'm leaving. That's how I roll.

Fair warning; do not take life too seriously. None of us are going to get out of here alive.

10-19-16

Mopping this house requires furniture/cage shuffling as I go. That being said, Felix's Dad sits on a posture ball rather than a chair at his computer desk. THAT being said I put that giant blue ball on top of his desk to mop.

This was Butters' goal for the day. Perching on a giant blue ball set on top of a desk. Cirque du Butterbean! This added 30 minutes to mopping because she wanted so badly to successfully land on that ball. And that ball rolled RIGHT off the desk every attempt.

Somebody had to spot that bird. Standing ovation for one Blue and Gold Macaw perched on a round blue ball on a computer desk!

10-21-16

Butters is back! (favoring me) Could it be the blue lightened up in my hair? Could it be Dad ever so slightly stepped away? Could it be she forgave me for leaving for New York? Could it be I don't care? Yeah, it's that last one. I am covered in Butters clingy, and I love it and I'm just happy I have my girl back.

Kirby has informed me he'll be staking out the dining/kitchen space to execute HALO landings on my shoulder when I come through now that Butters is hogging me in the office. By "informed me" I mean he scared the hahoo out of me just a minute ago when I went in the kitchen.

How many piggles does it take to demolish two handfuls of hay in 17 minutes? Two. In case you need to demolish two handfuls of hay in 17 minutes, now you know.

LeoBun, master of his domain, overlord of two floors of bunny condo, enforcer of hutch and hearth. Sometimes he's just a condo-nazi when it's time to swap towels and toys. I feel like I need a password to go upstairs and a receipt that I paid HOA fees.

Dear Home Depot; if your website says you have 7 of something I want, and you text me the location of said items in my chosen store via your website, and I call said store confirming said items, it would be really cool if the said items were actually there when I showed up. Not to say the two people standing around one aisle away weren't helpful with the "Hu., I guess we don't have it after all! Have you tried the 22nd Ave location?" It took your website, and 3 employees to totally not deliver your brand promise. Well played corporate giant. Well played.

It's a good thing I came home to a flock of parrots, two guinea pigs, a bun, two dogs and two lizards I really love otherwise I might be irritated. But I'm not. It's hard to be irritated when you have a macaw chuckling and sticking her tongue in your ear.

10-24-16

After much mulling and measuring and budgeting we decided to upgrade the Piggles CC Cage rather than spend $300 on the Piggles Casa de Hutch. Mostly because the Casa would get in my way of walking by and scooping up a piggles on the fly for a cuddle. We've expanded the Piggles Field to 5 feet by 2 and a half feet, added more deep bedding for digging, more toys and more boxes with different doors. Jamal-Pierre and Werthers are now totally exposed for all the cuddles I want to deliver at will. Win/win if you ask me. Most likely I'll expand upwards to a second floor with a ramp next year. They call that "progress" in real estate. Piggles now live in the dining room with LeoBun.

The dining room has now been renamed, " The Bun'n Piggles Cafe".

Fall in Florida; you get to open you windows for a few days! The best part of that part is the fresh air triggering parrot's scent. Butters gets so turned on by the open windows she releases a scent I like to call the smell of sunshine. Butters smells like sunshine, the house smells like sunshine. Oh but I do love open window Fall days.

10-25-16

Sugar is an inflammatory. It is. I'm not saying that, science said it. THAT being stated, whenever I start craving Entenmann's chocolate covered donuts I remember inflammation science, diabetes, and the hormonal affects of sugar. I hate science right now.

Felix has been working on his feet for about an hour now. He's on his tent, to my right, fastidiously working those tootsies. I asked him if his feet were a mess. He stopped his toe inspection, made a little parrot fist, looked at me and fartsound-chuckle-old man groaned me. I'm pretty sure I've just been scoffed at by a parrot.

Perfect Piggle Balance has been achieved in the new homestead. I put up a barrier dividing the homestead in half for Jamal-Pierre and Werthers. They just couldn't find their way to sharing a full space. It was too much to ask them to be in the same place and discuss things with care and concern. Sooner or later a subject came up and BLAM! Teeth Grinding. Like the Presidential debates.

Now that they can be together, see each other but do not have the responsibility of claiming things or territory they are new piggles! Happy, relaxed, lazy, and ready for head scratches and belly rubs. Werthers was the first to roll over to get a belly rub. He won a sweet pepper for that move.

10-27-16

Mid-afternoon snack; flax crackers smeared with raw peanut butter with cucumber slices on top. I can't eat any of that until I make portions for the flock. Skip the cucumbers, those are annoying. Felix happily licks a cracker chunk in his foods bowl. Butters eats hers on my shoulder leaving dactyly-peanuty-butter-toe prints on my shirt. Snickers sits on the sink faucet licking his like a lollypop dropping cracker bits missing peanut butter into the dishwater below. Kirby has his half a cucumber slice and cracker chunk with peanut butter in his Kirby bowl over on the kitchen table.

There. Everyone's happy. (parrot addendum; The Horde is not impressed with any of this) I make my portion and just as I'm about to chomp on this snack attack Kirby whizzes by my left ear careful to avoid Butters on my right and lands on the lip of the open peanut butter jar, cracker chunk in his beak.

I look at him. He looks at me.

"What?" I ask.

He drops his cracker chunk into the jar of peanut butter. He looks at me. The peanut butter I had smeared on his cracker chunk is mysteriously missing! He has no idea where it went.

10-28-16

Felix's dreaded weirdo neighborling is chopping branches off his oak tree while standing on his roof. He can see right into our house and the birds can see him. He's lopping heavy branches and when they hit his roof the thump is LOUD. One hour in, every companion in here is jumpy. I'm offering words of comfort with their names. "It's okay Snickers! It's okay Felix! It's okay Kirby!" etc. and so forth.

After 14 cycles of calling names and saying "it's okay", I forgot my dog's name. I went through four names until I could remember Turner's name.

"It's okay, Felix...er. no. KirbNO. Um. Butte...GAH! Leo...no. Turner, it's okay TURNER."

I am at maximum companion count for my brain.

I just spoke the words, "You have wings. I do not. Fly! I can't fly. Come here." I spoke these words sitting on the couch while holding out my hand as a landing zone. Snickers sat perched with one foot out asking me to help him off the cage door.

And so we just looked at each other, hand and foot out...staring at each other.

I lost the staring contest. I got up.

Snickers is on top of the domed macaw cage trying to have sex with a whole walnut. I say this simply to impress you.

It's that time of year. Shred the dead paperwork. Felix wanted to join in while I go through all our files to prune the paperwork. He's shredding his percentages of paper on the floor with me.

And he's skillfully learned how to make the shredder noise. He now is a professional parrot paper shredder.

I woke with the memory of a dream last night. I had been walking down a sidewalk in a city. The sidewalk was lined with a brick retaining wall and iron fence. I let my eyes follow the path of the brick retaining wall and listened to traffic and voices. So many voices in front of a hum of cars and city buses.

I came upon an African Grey parrot sitting on the retaining wall. He lifted a foot to ask for a ride. I obliged and turned around with a new thought to get to a car and drive home.

Issues after I wake up and think on these things:

The African Grey had poodle fur in African Grey colors and a Toucan beak.

The car we came to was the DeLorean from the Back to the Future movie. But Copper. Bright, shiny copper. The passenger seat was filled with parsley and one bright green cabbage.

I'm pretty sure this means, I need to buy some kimchee for me and parsley for the piggles. I called the African ToucaGrey Poodle, LittleGuy, in my dream. That means I'm going to meet some little guy selling kimchee and parsley. I'm going to Publix later, if I meet a little guy in the kimchee parsley aisle I'm going to ask him if he's seen Neo.

Felix doesn't care about any of my ponderings, he's eating uncooked organic egg pasta. Why, because he likes how it crackles when he eats it.

I've got all the macaw soft perches from the cages in the washing machine today. You know the "comfy perch" types. Snickers is going commando like repelling up and down the sides of the interior of his cage to eat and drink his breakfast offerings. Snickers is Rambo, like a boss.

Butters is sitting on top of her opened cage door. She's bemused that work will be involved to have breakfast. In fact, I'm pretty sure she's whining. She's flown over and landed on my shoulder twice to bonk my head in protest about this whole "have to climb the cage and hang on the side to eat out of bowls" thing. There are 5 other breakfast bowls on two other tree stands of course. But the idea I've left these 4 bowls in these two cages as an obstacle course is a total insult to her fragile state. She's Scarlet O'Hara in the potato field right now.

11-14-16

"There's no point to learning how to make patterns until you learn how to sew."

Grandma had a mouth full of straight pins, she was bent over her pattern table while I was busy on her sewing machine running straight lines of stitches up and down a practice cloth. She always taught me while I sewed. She never talked about sewing unless we were in her sewing room.

And you could never walk into her sewing room without shoes on. The carpet hid many a straight pin and missing needles.

Grandma taught me to use a sewing machine well. She taught me bias, and thread and cloth and settings on the machine. She taught me how to pin a pattern properly and cut it out cleanly. Alas Grandma died before she could teach me how to make my own patterns.

I still remember the smell of her sewing room. Clean fabrics of wool, cotton, rayon, polyester and such. Clean wool smells so good. The sewing room smelled of remnants of a hot steam iron, pattern papers, clean fabrics and the slightest bit of oil. She was always cleaning and oiling her sewing machine. I can still smell that room and the joy and contentment that surrounded us when we were together in it.

I took all my skills into Home Economics classes and left the teacher and other students behind. Whipping out an apron, oven mitt and table cloth before they finished cutting their patterns. The flip side to that is I hated cooking so the apron, oven mitt, and table cloth I made did not help my cause when we moved onto the kitchen area.

I bring Grandma's instruction to a very important emergency situation here. Snickers' favorite toy, "the girlfriend" as we like to call them, can not be purchased anymore. Oh, sure, I've tried bringing home variables that are "close" the the real thing. These offerings were quickly relegated to the replacement pile of rejection. Or what we like to call the pile of stuffed toys on top of Butters' cage.

Here's the thing, we can't just not have this toy in the house. These are girlfriends, and he needs them to relax. He also needs them to fly with, water board in all the water bowls, donk Butters in the head (I am assuming this is an offering of sorts, done poorly), drop, flop, flip, throw, and masturbate. This is serious. And we are down to the last two on earth, and they are really, REALLY, starting to show their age and, um....use.

So it's back to basics! Back to self sufficiency! Back to handling my own business, or his business.

Cali surprised me with a new sewing machine and all the accoutrements necessary to not only create needed items, but be creative in textile. I am totally excited. This weekend I created 3 new girlfriends for Snickers, tents for piggles, and a custom cage cover for Felix's bedroom cage.

All these projects did what Grandma ran out of time to do. Teach me how to create my own patterns. I think Grandma is laughing and enjoying watching me. And don't worry grandma, I washed my hands before working with the machine, and I cover it when I am done. Just like you taught me.

11-15-16

It sits alone on the cement pavers. Smoldering still, filled with repugnant waters of char and death. It's lived a long life. It served us well. It never faltered, waned or gave in to our demands. Until today.

It sits alone in the backyard a testament to fate itself and the distractions of a new sewing machine. My intent was benevolent. I only wanted to use it for an afternoon of pleasure with a beer whilst registering my new sewing machine. Yes, I've used it many times for this same 3-ish o'clock pleasure of the day. Until today.

Oh fate of dyslexic brain and nimble fingers! Oh ye fickle fat finger of time setting. OH! Fool that I am! Quickly I set the microwave timer as I had so many times before and then, even quicker did I dash up the stairs to my studio to read the serial number off my sewing machine. I bet I beat the microwave I had thought to myself!

It is to laugh!! Damn you serial number panel hidden like the great gold of Egyptian kings! Damn you and the dark room you reside! Well to be honest, I could have turned on the light in that room. But I have these vampire tendencies of never turning on lights. I'll wash dishes in a kitchen lit like dusk in the forest. I will crochet in only the flashing and changing lights of a television. Yes, I am vampire. Existing in twilight. I have no idea where that habit came from either.

But I digress.

Basically I'm in the studio more like 5 minutes and the microwave was set for 34 minutes not 3 minutes and 40 seconds.

I guess we should get that popcorn popper my husband and I were talking about earlier this week. That looked really cool. And fire proof.

11-18-16

Sciatica, with a side of Piriformis Syndrome and a dollop of Sacroiliac Joint troubles equals 48+ hours of long, painful, bedridden daydreaming, with a Lurker crawling all over your covers and pooping, but you can't move so you know what a statue in the city feels like.

Today I'm up, and thankful for a husband who can juggle better than me, and is so thoughtful on the little things that made this brutal episode tolerable and manageable while it was definitely the worst.

For a California King number bed that let me change settings, groan and roll around like a walrus giving birth and generally offered room for bedridden paraphernalia.

For rice bags delivering moist heat, and ice packs to chill the pain and a refrigerator and microwave that makes those items work.

For NEW popcorn popping bowls arriving while I'm bedridden! Whoot! And of course Cali ordered two bowls, because he's smart like that. I'm just cheap, I would've just ordered one.

For a flock that is so good, no matter what happens. Dad could work from home, take care of me, and herd the circus with not too much fuss. Except for the morning we woke up to the Horde flying around because their flight aviary didn't get closed the night before. And once THAT genie is out of the bottle, that's that for the day.

For coffee I couldn't drink for 2 days and missed. I miss it just for the ethereal comfort it delivers. I had a nice cup today.

For the crazy daydream ideas I gained while laying there breathing through the pain. I painted 3 paintings in my head, and came up with a CRAZY good idea for sculpting that I can't even say out loud here cause I am going to do it.

And I am thankful for the ability to hear my flock, companions and husband work together in my absence. Seriously, hearing his voice and their responses, lifted my heart. I married well.

I'm off to the number bed and rice packs to let a little blue bird nurse my care, and probably poop on me a couple times. I'm sure it's good medicine though.

11-21-16

A LeoBun throwing Dixie cups is saying, "Come Hither! I am ready to be entertained by your lowbrow humor!"

A LeoBun banging a wood block is saying, "Come Hither! What is this empty BunFoods bowl? I am insulted and aghast."

A LeoBun running in circles, dashing up the ramp, and falling sideways in front of the second story door window is saying, "Come Hither! I am prepared to allow you to worship my cuteness by applying the BunBrush of Adoration. Mind the gap."

A LeoBun throwing himself into his hay box is saying, "Be Gone! I have no time for your silliness. I must nap on this timothy hay and dream the dream of Buns."

A LeoBun banging his water bottle is saying, "I am a dehydrating bored Bun!"

Leo is a simple Bun.

11-22-16

LeoBun putting his wood block in his empty BunFoods Bowl is saying, "I have no faith in you now."

The best laid plans of mice and parrot toy makers. Oh sure you THINK it's a hanging toy. Go ahead and spend 3 hours tying little knots to hold toys and blocks in a precise order and distance. Go ahead and do that.

Silly human.

Interesting finding on said hanging toy that is not hanging anymore. The totality of the parts covers more square footage than wall to wall carpeting.

Our neighbors have a new puppy. He's an American Boxer. Totally adorable, and totally left alone in the backyard calling for contact and to find his pack. He is so upset he sounds like someone is cleaning glass with alcohol rags...squeaking rather than yipping. His collar is too snug on his neck. I sat with him for a few minutes and we visited each other through the fence. I told him he was a good boy. That I loved him. That he was so handsome. And I gave him a few kibbles from our Blue Mountain food stuffs.

Then as I got up I proclaimed with an overly loud comment, "Baby, if you were my new companion you wouldn't be alone in an overgrown dirty backyard."

Ironically, 3 minutes back in our house with our companions and I no longer hear window cleaning cries of an adorable puppy.

There's a big blue chicken on my shoulder preening her chest feathers and scratching her head. There is magic in the light breathing of a parrot. I can hear her breath and soft purr of satisfaction as she details her feather collection.

Felix is kvetching about juice while cracking his pasta pieces. I'd suggest he drink his water, but that would just lead to an argument about warm tea and the lack thereof.

Snickers is eating a date like a boss. He takes his dates seriously. I respect his commitment on the matter.

Butters and Snickers love having Makarate matches when I vacuum. The noise and vibration gets them all fired up.

When I turn off the vacuum to move furniture out of the way, they both freeze in their Makarate position and wait for the noise to start.

For fun I'll start and stop the vacuum randomly just to see them freeze with their feet joined, head feathers all helmet head and both looking at me with tongues hanging out in anticipation. It's like that old game of Red Rover. But with parrots and a vacuum. And no real finish line.

My vacuuming won't finish, they're out of their cages Makarating.

Life isn't an Ever Lasting Gobstopper. It was never intended to stay the same while never ending.

12-2-16

Today the City of St Petersburg begins milling and resurfacing our street. Heavy equipment, trucks etc. rumble passed our home in orderly fashion. The milling machine is pretty impressive to watch. I'm surprised how quiet it is.

I'm also surprised by how excited two macaws can be watching trucks and a milling machine. They are far louder than that milling machine. Snickers is using a new word in celebration of his milling machine running up and down his street.

"WOW! Snickerdoodlewow!!"

Butters has chosen the Diva Route and is just screaming at the trucks calling them Snickers.

If anyone should ever ponder the question; Are macaws louder than an operating road milling machine and 5 yelling men? The answer is yes, by a good percentage of "WHAT!?!? I can't hear you!"

12-5-16

We have two Leopard Geckos. Rotini and Donotelli Gambini. Rotini laid two perfect eggs in the water bowl this morning and has spent the last 3 hours filling the water bowl with sand and excavator clay to bury her nest of two. She's still at it, but with less verve. She circles her mound and then fills in spaces only she can see as imperfections. Like an artist, not sure if their creation is finished.

Donotelli is at the highest rock formation looking down as she does her burial work. He's not moved an inch all this time. I can't tell if he's Project Manager or staying out of the way.

After all this birthing and burying business she's going to be hungry and sleepy over the next couple of days. That girl can pack some mealworms when she wants.

This reminds me of my experiences in motherhood. I was so tired and hungry after both kids. I could have eaten the whole of what the hospital cafeteria offered, but I was too tired. I never wanted to bury the kids in sand though. At that time.

12-6-16

My sister is amazing. You should know this. She needed a warm body to scan for images to obtain certification on a CT scanner in St Pete. I support my sister in all her endeavors, I am that warm body.

I have a brain. For all those claiming otherwise, I SAW MY BRAIN. And my sister burned that image to disc for evidence. So that debate is now settled.

12-8-16

Everybody has a price. They may act as though they don't. They'll pitch fits, refuse to cooperate or negotiate or discuss the immovable moral belief system that beats deep in the center of their hearts and souls. Their line in the sand is welded steel in marble and encased in unobtainium.

Until you give them a belly rub for 20 minutes, and then not only can you trim a piggle's toenails, but you could paint them raving red.

Raving Red would match his eyes if I did that last bit.

12-9-16

I've got 2 pounds of blue and gold dork hanging off my shirt collar by a beak, she's pulled it over my shoulder and down along my arm. She's just hanging by one foot egging me on to get into the bird room. Pointing with one reaching foot while dangling by my elbow.

I type, she tugs. I look down. She looks up and reaches toward the room filled with her favorite foods. Obviously she can't eat alone today.

And by the sounds of things hitting the floor in there, Snickers can.

The last 2 days the road resurfacing guys have been very eager to get to work. 5:30 in the morning eager.

Kirby is fast asleep on top of the cockatiels' flight, back to the window, red beak hidden in a soft mound of shoulder feathers.

He'd be doing that on my shoulder if Butters wasn't currently trying to get me out of my parked space in front of this computer.

12-12-16

Washing the dog's water bowl is an event for Kirby. It is literally a "thing" for him. He gets so excited while I'm washing that one bowl. He climbs up, down, and all around my shirt front, hangs upside down to get as close as possible to the bowl in my hands, walks out to my hand via my forearm to inspect my work and spends a good amount of time pretending to bath.
You see he's like Felix. He's a water bowl bather. But not just any bowl. It has to be THIS bowl. And it has to be this bowl right after I've washed it. Set on the T that separates the two sinks. Filled with cold filtered water direct from the fridge.

In this place, time and status Kirby can get his bath on.

I sometimes just let the dogs drink the water when he's done. My own personal inside joke.

The road crew finished all their repaving work on our street yesterday. Snickers misses all the trucks. He's just sitting on the window sill flock calling the crew and growl pouting their absence.

We hit a snag in the phonebook acquisitions department around here a few months back. CVS no longer has them for free at the front door of the store. Felix was not impressed with technical books from Microsoft. His demolition skills were waning from lack of demo work. But, Dad to the rescue with a great idea! Children's coloring books. They offer just the right paper weight and texture for Felix Demolition. To show his approval Felix is currently shredding and tearing pages out of his tent onto my office floor.

And Butters is so very kind to fly over and send them into the bird room via air mail.

I feel sorry for our Bruiser Bear. He can't help it he's old and dazed. He can't help it he likes eating piggle poop. He is a victim of his own obsessions really. He searches tirelessly to find those lost and forgotten morsels from past piggle condo cleanings. The joy on his face when he discovers just one; well it just breaks your heart really. Oh, if only I didn't have a gag reflex, he could feast on that which he loves until his very last breath.

But alas...EW! Piggle poop breath!

That space in time where your macaw hasn't done the morning poop yet and has chosen to burrow in your bed blankets first. Then sticks his head out from under said blankets, laughs at you, and you think he's working up that waddle, but he's not. Then he disappears under the blankets again, laughing at you.

Not cool Snickers.

LeoBun has decided the only recreational opportunity for today is kicking all his bedding out of the Condo while growling like a little beastie. He has followed this up with binky, ramp run, binky, ramp run, slam a water bottle, toss a toy. Binky. This could be Morris Code.

I have roughly five statements made by flock clients that I can't get out of my head. One that gnaws on my heart quietly like a tapeworm is "He's just so RESTRICTING!!!" (caps and punctuation applied by the email writer, not me). Restricting. I stand here typing with a big blue chicken on my right shoulder, a Felix to my right napping on a Felix tent, a Kirby on my left wrist lusting over the keys I am busy tapping, songs of cockatiels fill the house and a gorgeous male Scarlet we named Snickers enjoying breakfast nearby on his favorite breakfast spot.

I find my world expanded, softened, elevated, challenged and celebrated because of our companions.

It's the unreasonable expectations that are restricting. Parrots or no.

Snickers has me using "the mom voice". Something I honed back in my human parenting phase. I've decided he's most like my son at 2 and half years of age.

"S-n-i-c-k-e-r-s...stop." I deliver this with the "looking over the glasses with authority" look. Which is stupid on my part, he's not looking at me.

"HUH?" He scrambles to a different location with a look of shock and surprise and "Who me?" on his face.

I find his dramatic executions solid enough to carry the moment, but I doubt he could carry a full length feature film.

12-16-16

Ten Cute Things at my House Right Now;

1) A Felix, half asleep on his tent keeping half an eye on my doings.

2) One piggle, specifically his butt hanging out of his hide box. Piggle butts are adorable.

3) Another piggle, splayed out asleep belly side down. Piggle Food Coma.

4) A Gecko, currently scratching his head on a rock trying to get his shed started.

5) A LeoBun, pushing his empty food bowl around like a shopping cart. I can't hear his message through all that cute.

6) A Kirby, buzzing in my ear and delivering kissysmacks down my ear canal. That last part is cute, but loud.

7) A Snickers and Butters morning meeting. They are agreeing on details over there, things could go sideways.

8) Five Muscovy Ducks, in our front yard, being ducks.

9) Teeny Tiny Turner and Bruiser, our dogs, asleep in their favorite spots, that are totally in the way.

10) A Horde, chirpachatting about the minutes from their last meeting.

Snickers learned how to say my "GAH!" His enunciation is impeccable.

He just spent 10 minutes throwing everything out of a tree stand bowl while hollering, "GAH!"

Pellet Splash.
"GAH!"
Pellet Splash.
"GAH! hahahaha oh snickerdoodles."
Pellet Splash.
"GAH! GAH! uhOh! hahaahaha SNICKers!"

Now the house is filled with the sound of dog toe nails clicking on the wooden surface of the tree stand's tray, because it all fell down there JUST for Bruiser.

12-29-16

Pain. It is the great Diviner. I'm not talking about the hammer on toe kind. I mean the incessant, constant acute kind that's ebb is slightly under the feeling of a steak cleaver embedded in your back. It's high pitch; reminiscent of the hatching scene in the movie Alien. Never ending, it pulses and prods and challenges you to think about anything else. This is the pain that proves a person's make and model, as my grandpa would say.

My muse is not a complaint. It's an observation. I've given birth in both available fashions. I've been hit by a car while riding a motorcycle. I have been assaulted. I already met pain. Or so I thought. I knew all those pains would end. Today I don't know about this one. I can't say. My doctor won't say and my physical therapist brushes off the question like a seasoned politician.

What I do know is Kirby has learned how to ride me like a rolling log on a river while I convalesce in this bed with ice then heat. No matter how I roll over, crawl around or move my pained self that bird never falls off and always stays on top of me. His new favorite game is simply walking my radius as I barrel roll from one side of the bed to the other. And on a California King he gets two and a half good rotations. He's smart about it, choosing my waist as his walkway. I am his personal Jungle Gym Log Roll, albeit smelling of BenGay.

I suppose once all this is over, and I finally suss out the issues of piriformis, gluteus, et al, he'll want this game to continue.

Which will totally happen.

2017

As a Floridian I can testify Winter is about 4 days long. And it's not really winter. It's weather just long enough to force you to run your heater. But not long enough to get rid of that smell your heater gives off for it's first few uses. December 2016 converted to January 2017 as a warmer winter than normal. We didn't run the heater. I just added blankets.

The winter of 2016 was a 6 blanket winter. The Summer of 2016 was a 2 blanket summer for me so, it wasn't that cold at all.

Winter into Spring in Florida offers a short time where being outside isn't a sauna experience. You get a few hours of open windows without the humidity turning your house into a fish bowl. You also get the most amazing few days of growth on oak trees. One day they are dark green to brown. Next they are covered in thousands of light green buds bursting into the smallest of leaves.

We do have four seasons in Florida, believe it or not. Three of them last about 3 weeks in total is all.

Felix has taken to dancing at his fast through pass through window. We humans call that the pass through over the kitchen sink. Felix calls it his Disco Floor. He particularly enjoys a good dance off when Dad or I are washing dishes. He gets his head twisting off it's joint so fast and furious I'm pretty sure he has Metallica playing in his head.

He added a new step series to his move and continued the most adorable Disco Heavy Metal Dance Off to date. So cute.

Until he launched himself off the fast through pass through window onto the sprayer with extreme vengeance and fury. Gallo Enojado of the Lucha Libre de Florida needs no juala to fight! Gallo Enojado only requires the site of his arch nemesis! Filthy pig sprayer! His moves fatal, his ire raw, Gallo Enojado clawed sprayer into submission.

His finish signature move; dump his own breakfast bowl on top of Sprayer in disgust and insult.

Filthy Pig Sprayer.

1-3-17

Turtles can't think around corners. All the turtles behind our house living in Tinney Creek walk our backyard fence line fervently trying to go under or around the fence to get to the lake across the street. Here's the thing; They could literally walk a straight unimpeded line from the creek to the lake. Yet their little turtle GPS settings are off. They walk to our fence and they walk the fence line testing the fence every so often trying to go under it.

This sets Butters off like a Tornado siren. There is no going off until that turtle has walked roughly 100 feet of fence line out of Butters' sight. And obviously the turtle is hurling insults at Butters the entire time.

Today was T-Day. The unthinkable happened. A turtle made it under the fence and proceeded to march straight at Butters, hurling looks and insults through the window along the way.

Butters lost her marbles. Snickers decided to loose his with her. Felix calmly walked into his tent yelling "BAD BIRD!" and Kirby continued to preen. Lurkers do not care about turtles.

I ran outside as all momma bears do when their babies are being insulted and threatened. As I picked this large paper plate sized turtle up I watched 2 chicken sized macaws screaming at me through the window. "Put it down! Don't! You'll die! Stop!" I'm sure that's what they were yelling.

I brought the turtle into the house. Of course this is a wild creature, and I'm not doing any friendly introductions, but I am showing the chickens that turtles smell like brackish water and are benign. Albeit rude and obnoxious.

Butters turned off her Tornado Turtle Siren and flew over to take a close look at the evil that cometh from the depths of Tinney Creek. Turtle returned the inspection by sticking his head out and attempting to ambulate.

TORNADO TURTLE SIREN ENGAGE!

I took the poor guy that can't think around corners outside to the front yard, pointed his face to the lake and bid him farewell.

Butters bid him good riddance.

1-6-17

Mornings are a cacophony of messaging around here. So many personalities vying for control of my brain and intent as I walk down the stairs. Two dogs panting at the top and bottom of the stairs, wanting to go out and eat breakfast at the same time. A rabbit thumping and throwing toys reminding me green beans are next and he is first in the next. Thankfully Felix is in the shower with Dad discussing important matters. The macaws and Kirby are still asleep in their roost cages. Jamal-Pierre piggles looks up at me as I turn the corner into the dining room. Or what we like to call Piggles'n Bun Cafe. Jamal is a pragmatic piggles. He knows a simple standing and chewing on the cage wire fervently will move breakfast along. We have a good relationship he and I.

And then there is Werthers, destined for stage and screen. We should move to Los Angeles so he can further his career. He's too old to get into the Disney entertainment machine here in Florida.

I greet every one individually with good mornings and a bit of a head rub for acknowledgments. Werthers is last. He is writhing on the floor of his condo. Calling out hunger pains and starvation. He kicks over his hide, slings hay and falls down on his face only to look up at me dragging his dead legs behind him as he claws his way toward me in a fervent call for sustenance. He is on the brink of death, nay! He IS dead! Only parsley can bring him back from the Pearly Gates now.

His body lies still, except for the whining, breathing and running in circles part. That was obviously a last gasp kind of thing. Yes, he is going to die of starvation as he has not eaten for at least 2 minutes. Curse the hay! Curse and reject that bowl of pellets! Turn your back on hay treats and squares! LIES! WITCHCRAFT! FALSE HOPE all!!

WHERE. IS. THE. PARSLEY.

Again he falls face first into a mound of useless first cutting timothy hay. Hopeless, forlorn and facing death alone in this dark, cold world.

And yet! I open the fridge door and life springs eternal driving this manipulative actor of a piggles to the side of the cage like a WWE wrestler proclaiming his greatness before a title fight!

ME FIRST!!!!!

Sorry kid, coffee first. I was just getting the creamer.

1-6-17

I brought a private patio fantasy to Florida from Illinois in 1999. I thought all patios and decks in Florida were always perfect all the time. Happy, bright, clean and waiting for revelers to join them in the sun.

Actually Florida patios not protected by a Florida room type enclosure are always sandy, and dirty to one degree or another. The wind just brings in all that particle stuff from the Gulf and Tampa Bay in our area. After a few years of fighting that truth I realized the best practice was simply creating a scenario easily hosed off. I tip and lean the chairs up against the table so the seats don't collect traveling sands and soil from the shores not far away.

Our daughter was down from Illinois for a short visit to see family and friends. I miss her. She came over and we sat on the patio and talked and talked for what felt like 3 minutes, but really turned out to be hours.

I can't bare to tip these two chairs back up. I see us talking in them. They make me smile.

1-8-17

There's a comfort, inexplicable. She rests heavy on my shoulder but her whispers and purrs are weightless. I had intended on going upstairs and doing a bit of arting. I had intended on sewing, sculpting and the like in celebration of my back letting go and giving way to less pain.

But you see, Butters saw me standing in the darkened office typing away. Just me, catching up on parrot consultations, emails and the like. The clicking was too inviting for her. She is my office assistant. The house is quiet, except for the campaign raging on XBox in the bird room. Yes, Felix likes Dad and his XBox.

Snickers is busy with his girlfriends transporting them back and forth and back and forth between cages and treetops.

Kirby is asleep one foot up with a full crop on top of the Horde's aviary. We shared lunch and he is in full digest mode.

So here I am half asleep, with a Butters purring in my ear and preening that ear randomly. How can I move? How can I break this bond simply to go art?

I can't. I'm stuck here with inexplicable comfort on one shoulder. This is the best stuck ever.

1-9-17

Mine is not to question why, mine is but to do or die. Or more specifically encourage what works and remove what doesn't.

I make girlfriends for Snickers. He's got his taste in girls, too. Round, soft, colorful and preferably with handles. I don't question the why, I just enjoy Snickers enjoying his girls. They travel together, eat together, nap together and ultimately they get water boarded. Again, I ask no questions.

When Snickers is feeling really happy he tries to share his girlfriends with Felix or Butters by dangling girlfriend oh so carefully over the edge of their cage and trying to hit Felix or Butters in the head with her. This is ambassadorship at it's finest.

He's less than finessing all this sharing though. Hollering "uhOH!" while blindly wielding her up and down and up and down and I can't guarantee he's aiming at anything at all.

I can guarantee neither Butters or Felix are interested in this sharing moment. Butters screams, flashes and takes off in an opposite direction. Felix yells out his angry old man grumble followed by the accusations of "BAD BIRD! BAD BAD BAD BIRD STOP!"

Snickers takes off after Butters, Butters takes off to my shoulder and Felix is hanging upside down in his cage ringing his Anti-Dactyl bell with extreme prejudice.

I'd consider all this removable if it weren't for one simple fact. Felix's Anti-Dactyl bell is a Dactyl Attracter Bell and he knows it. It's also a Round Counting Bell.

Round Three just got called.

I only think I know what I'm doing, which is the pinnacle symptom of confused. So says Felix. Mornings are Felix's time to fix my thinking and execution about breakfast during the 1 hour we have alone before the rest of the crew comes downstairs. He is my tutor.

Dad brings Felix down, sets him on the fast through pass through window over the sink. It is here he expects all bowls to be filled, finished and ready for his inspections. If I've not gotten this done before he gets set down I hear about it. "HERE!", "Applepopcorn HERE!" "Hereherehere Juice?", "Hey. Here!"

Being berated by a bird before coffee is exhausting.

Once inspections are concluded, Felix begins his breakfast in the fast through pass through. Phase One of eating starts here at ground zero. I've been in boot camp training with this phased eating locations for a few months. Generally when he's ready to move all his bowls to his cage, and go into Phase Two he'll just stop eating, stare at me and rapid fire "here!" until I offer a step up transport. Mom Taxi can be slow on the uptick, it's true.

And that's where my boot camp training was stuck. Felix was not getting a quick enough response from me when he hailed his taxi service for Phase Two.

He picked up the training pace yesterday by threatening to throw his food bowl off the fast through pass through and into the sink. But for the grace of Dirty Pig Sprayer, I would have a sink full of everything Felix loves. Or loved. I suppose you can't love it if it's not delivered properly. There's a lesson somewhere in there for me.

I ran around the corner and found Felix tapping his foot in expectation, while delivering the Eye of Disdain. He stood over the precariously perched food bowl for extra dramatic effect. Immediately without any conversation I extended my hand and he hopped on and off we, and his food bowls, headed to the top of his cage.

Lesson delivered.

Today he merely picked up the edge of his food bowl and banged it against the fast through pass through over and over and over while yelling with a beak full of bowl edge, "HEY! Here! here! here!" Which sounded like "her! her! her!"

I ran around the corner, and found Felix with a beak full of bowl edge threatening a dump it all off into the sink.

"Seriously Fee?" I realized I'd been trained.

"It's all right." His response let me know he knew that already.

1-11-17

There's a fine line between teaching and hazing.

I arrive to my morning lessons with Felix with a positive attitude, slightly drowsy, but positive. Food bowls filled and ready for inspections. Coffee on the way, piggles and bun eating parsley, dog bellies filled. Today I'm ready.

Dad brings Felix down and sets him on the pass through fast through, we do our morning meeting on today's events, how we slept and shake our heads at the old dogs doing old dog things on the floor. He drinks his blend, I small talk Felix. And then it's a kiss and a goodbye at the front door. Felix bids Dad farewell in a happy voice, "HELLO!"

It's time for today's inspections and lesson!

I walk back into the kitchen and find the Professor holding his larger food bowl by the edge, slightly tipping the bowl up. I stop walking. He lifts it a bit more. I take a step forward, " Felix...don't do it."

He tilts his head with the bowl in beak asking a simple question, "What?"

The bowl flies into the sink with a crash and a scattering sound of contents.

He has this chuckle that sounds like a George Bush Jr laugh on Saturday Night Live. He tops it off with a fart sound and stuffs his head in the smaller food bowl George Chuckling all the while.

George Chuckling with a full mouth is incredibly rude.

1-12-17

"Rabbit! What are you doing rabbit?!?" That's my morning invitation to some roughhousing in the condo while I clean and set his breakfast up.

46

Leo dashes out of his tent hide area and makes a NASCAR turn flinging bedding everywhere and through the cage mesh. He lands a big binky hop right in front of the open door, and looks me square in the eye.

I wait for his answer. Leo throwing Dixie cups is a yes. Leo throwing an empty breakfast bowl is obviously a no.

Dixie cups fly! Let the games begin!

LeoBun loves roughhousing, I mess up his bedding and throw his toys around, he growls runs up to my hands, digs, knocks his toys out of my hands, throws those toys, growls, binkies and then just drops into a flat pancake for petting and brushing. I brush him, gently pull on his ears, rub his feet, rub his belly sides, and then BAM!

It's on like Donkey Kong! He jumps straight up in the air, runs a NASCAR lap around the condo and slides back into my waiting hands to growl and throw Dixie cups while I push around bedding and grab toys from him and growl back. He succumbs to the need to be adored and brushed and falls into my hands for same.

We cycle through this about 3 times and then he's serious about eating.

I go about my cleaning and he goes about his eating while dismissing me with a loud and serious THUMP! of his big too cute for words back foot.

I'm pretty sure my rabbit is a dictator. A really cute, soft, warm, doe eyed dictator.

1-13-17

That purr. That purr in my ear and warm weight leaning into my cheek pretty much pays forward whatever is falling down my shirt. Like walnut shell shrapnel.

There's a pile of walnut dust and shell shrapnel building at my feet as well.

Like the show Gold Rush, when they have that pile of rock building up under the conveyor belt and everyone is running around yelling that it's getting too close to the belt. Shouts of "Where's the loader!?!?" and "Get Rick over here!"

Obviously Butters got her gold out of the pay dirt.

I need to shake out all the shrapnel from my shirt. It's building up and rather itchy. But she's gruxing now, one foot holding my ear. Snickers just landed on the desk and crawled up my shrapnel filled shirt to sit on my forearm. Now he's preening looking out the window watching the neighbor across the street work on his bright orange muscle car.

He revs his Pontiac's engine, Snickers is duly impressed letting out a growl.

I'm typing with one hand.

Felix has just begun exploding his coloring book in his tent to my right. The perfectly shaped coloring book shrapnel doesn't stay in his tent but rather lands on the pile of walnut and walnut shell over burden on the floor.

My shirt itches, typing with one hand, and I can no longer see my right foot for all the black and white coloring book art. A mound of cartoon collateral damage.

I love my life.

1-17-17

"We wait, starving for moments of high magic to inspire us, but life is a banquet of common enchantment waiting for our alchemists' eyes to notice." excerpt; "Blessed are the Weird". Jacob Nordby.

In goes a pistachio. A cashew follows with a plop. He's watching every move I make only an inch away from the bowl's edge. If he had a notepad, he'd be making those notes at this point.

I fish for another cashew, not whole, a half. And not broken as that will not do. Plop. I drop an apple chunk in next. I look at Felix, he looks back. Yes Fee, I laugh to myself, there is only ONE red side to those six sides of apple chunk.

I run back to the kitchen, I forgot something. Felix's voice follows me from behind, "POPCORN!"

I return with the pasta, dry, tubular, organic, egg-based and mini. He watches them rattle to the bottom of the building snack attack pile at the bottom of his white food bowl.

"How's that look Felix?" I ask with growing confidence, if not a bit of parenting parrot pride.

He steps forward, looks down, looks up and delivers his verdict, "It's alright."

Gosh, calm down Felix. I wouldn't know what to do with any more enthusiasm.

He waits. I look back. What's the issue? I have my bowl of popcorn, he has his bowl of everything important and inspection certified. I churn the contents of his afternoon snack attack.

"What? You've got the cashews, apple, pasta and pistachio what's the deal Fee....oh." I blush.

"POPCORN." His look is stern and yet forgiving. Obviously knowing this was coming as it had yesterday at about this time.

I reached left with my right hand and grabbed warm kernels from my own bowl and dropped them into Felix's bowl to my right.

"POPCORN!" *lipsmack sounds* Beak on popcorn crunches proceeded in glee. I just watched and laughed with pleasure to see him so happy over something so simple and plain. He loves his popcorn.

"What?" He asked, while still filling his beak with warm moist kernels. He never lifts his head out of a bowl once the feed is on.

"Nothing Felix. You are just so hilarious. I love you." I turn back to my keyboard and grab a few kernels for myself, out of my bowl of course.

fartsound *George Bush Jr chuckle*

1-18-17

I spy with my little eyes...

Rabbit ears tipping, swaying, straightening, flexing, widening, contracting and pointing the way to that rabbit's next thought.

An African Grey Parrot, exotic and not meant for this place. Yet he perches contentedly cleaning talons of fury and straightening feathers that have moved out of place. Stretching wing and shoulder he recites his collection of human forms of sounds and language. I see and hear this and think how fortunate am I.

A coffee cup empty, and in the kitchen a half filled french press waiting to fill it. But I can't go to the kitchen. There is a blue and gold macaw on my shoulder half asleep, gruxing herself into REM.

A small wooden sign, that reminds me, "Be BRAVE" in bright white paint. This has become easier as days go by.

A small shiny Lego Batman holding even smaller batarangs in each Lego hand. I snapped him together and the evil mechanical Ion Inducer of Death that he has to destroy, just the other day. I like certain toys. Because toys remind me to be childlike in a world that would prefer I worry over itself. A child only thinks of magic and possibilities. A child does not worry about boundaries unknown.

A magnificently colored Scarlet Macaw. Carefully splashing, tossing and throwing food out of food bowls because that's what he does. Snickers is a constant reminder of the words written by Abraham Maslow, "What one can be, one must be."

Again, how fortunate am I.

1-20-17

It's 3:30 in the afternoon. I've a finished bowl of popcorn to my left. It is not alone either. There's an empty beer bottle to the left of it.

I have a macaw preening my cheek and purring on my right shoulder. Another in his cage asleep (his door is open, yet he prefers to nap inside) and Felix preening after a water bowl bath of EPICness. His cage and under it looks like that monsoon scene from the movie Jumanji. I'll need two towels to wipe up the floor. And one more for what I missed under the tree stand.

I've vacuumed the entire house except the bird room. The vacuum with it's trailing unplugged cord snaking on the floor is testimony. It sits declaring my guilt from afar. Even in my peripheral vision I see it's damning shadow. VACUUM! It's silence is so loud.

But I'm rather full, and the Heineken has cut the edge off that ridiculous "go get'm attitude", succubus that it is. I'd rather mess about in graphics and write words that I hope are funny. Thank you very much.

VACUUM!! A hellish hissing voice with no sound, just a shadow in my right eye's corner.

Shut up ShopVac.

I can't vacuum until I wipe up the Felix Bath Fest of 2017. Woodstock was easier to straighten out than this slog fest. I'm exhausted just thinking about that extra step.

VACUUM!!!

SHUT. UP. SHOPVAC. Seriously. What's the point? I'll clean up Felix Bath Fest of 2017, sweep and vacuum and we STILL HAVE macaws! You are so stupid ShopVac. I may as well brush my teeth with peanut butter. None of this really makes sense.

ShopVac sits in silence. Because he knows, oh yes, he knows what comes of his demands. A full belly, wheezing tubes, and being pulled into furniture for not cooperating with my advanced dragging techniques. Sooner or later he's going to eat that table leg as I groan out loud because I have to unplug from one side of the room to finish the other side. Because Snickers can not control his need to make sure everything that is destroyed in his cage, lands outside of his cage.

Butters' side is easier. Diva's do not destroy, they just admire themselves in the reflection of the window while adjusting feathers.

It's 3:50 and Butters is chuckling and preening my neck. I'm certain she's letting me know vacuuming is futility with suction.

1-24-17

You know your dog is old when he doesn't even bother committing the crime, he just gets caught considering it then turns around and walks away. I can literally hear the angst filled grandpa grumpy mumble echoing in his skull. Busted before the commission again.

It's like the movie Minority Report. I'm Tom Cruise with a hologram crime computer interface, also known as Bruiser's Face Contemplating Bowl Jacking Turner's Breakfast. It's very high tech. It's the minute Bruiser won't look me in the eye and his bowl is empty. Again, very high tech stuff.

I accidentally left the aviary door open after putting foraging toys in for the Horde. You put Grape Nuts cereal in the foraging bowl and you get reverse thrust on 4 cockatiels. In case you need to get 4 Horde members back in their genie bottle.

Crunching cockatiels of success Batman!

1-26-17

Kirby sleeps in a hammock. Once upon a time, for 2 weeks, he slept perched on a wooden dowel perch. But it lasted 1 week. He chewed it to bits at night. I installed a second and it went down in the fiery flames of beak chipper action as well. So, I crocheted a little 14 inch X 4 inch hammock out of soft jute yarn. That was 4 years ago. Over time he's installed windows in his hammock to look through the right and left. I can't really say why considering we're discussing his bedroom roost which he likes covered for sleeping. But hey, aren't we all a little DIY HGTV?

Today I began crocheting a new hammock. It'll take a day or two depending on things. I'll wash it in scent free detergent, dry it in the sunny fresh air and work it to be soft around the edges where he sets his feet to sleep. I'll carefully hang it in the exact same way and location. Fresh, clean, soft and welcoming.

And he could see it, shriek with terror and go whizzing downstairs to hide in the dish rack next to the sink.

It's a crap shoot around here sometimes.

Felix is carefully and determinedly trying to pull the small nails out of his tent tree stand this morning. He grabs the edge of his tent towel to protect his beak and then grabs that little nail and wiggles the nail loose. He never tries to just pull on the nails before wiggling them. And he never does any of this without the towel in his mouth. And he uses the fat hemmed edge, not the thin edge.

When someone asks if Felix "can talk", I laugh and answer, "Talk? This bird project plans and executes with safety protocols."

1-26-17

Things I've had to say out loud today:

Felix does not want your girlfriend!

Put that down.

Leave that alone.

Come here.

Don't throw all your food out.

What are you doing over there.

Don't touch the outlet.

Butters does not want your girlfriend!

I bring out all these toys, and you play with a napkin off the floor.

Stop eating the house!

Public Service Announcement:
Don't have parrots? Think you want a parrot? Here's a simple test. Do you really like kids? You'll like a parrot. Do you find children annoying, loud and destructive? Get a houseplant.

1-28-17

I just finished hanging a dozen new employment opportunities in the macaw's cages. They are both filled with hanging glorious whatnots of chipper material. Joined with colorful wooden bridges and slinging swings.

Snickers jumps on the window blinds instead.

Butters prefers a leftover C hook.

Tough crowd.

1-30-17

Day 2 Death Toll; Snickers has murdered two of the dozen new employment opportunities. As is his modus operandi he found the single weakest spot of two identical toys and assassinated them both with two snips of a beak. Now we have 10 new foot toys!

Felix is molting pretty good. His downy feathers, and smaller red and white buttfeathers always go first. In the morning the towel at the bottom of his roost cage is covered in a Felix snow storm. Snickers is currently a bit roosty. Every morning he needs to go into Felix's roost cage to muck about and pretend he found the perfect tree for raising a family. This requires reworking the towel to accommodate his pretend wife. That requires rolling around, towel shoveling with his head and general physical mayhem.

Snickers came out of Felix's roost cage wearing a downy feather boa and matching downy buttfeather hat today. FabuLOUS!

LeoBun is running up and down his ramp, THUMPing the second story floor and throwing Dixie cups at the door like a Triple A pitcher. He either wants a new towel, wants more hay, or wants the first floor cleaned for the new bedding. I need to make him a "Housekeeping Needed" sign to hang on the front of his hutch. Or maybe just a butler bell. Although, I've already got bell ringing demanders around here. I should just stick with signage.

2-1-17

Working on edits in the book I have Snickers on my head, Butters right behind me on the tree stand, Felix on his tent to my right and Kirby on his secret perch to my left. The Horde are quietly eating fresh endive and spinach. This house is quiet. Except for one member.

Jamal-Pierre is beating the business out of his water bottle. His water bottle is now a toy and he is just belligerently throwing it back and forth and banging in on the side of the coral. And making a hilarious sound that I THINK is a growl. He has only one goal. Get rid of all the water.

Because mom doesn't have anything else to do but fill Jamal-Pierre's water bottle boxing toy. Nope. Not one other thing.

2-2-17

If you haven't found a reason to laugh today. Consult your local companion parrot. Parrots are professional funny bone locators.

Every morning is like opening Christmas packages around here. Snickers, Kirby and Butters are the last to get up in the morning and wait patiently, if not sleepily, in their bedroom roost cages to be uncovered and released into their day. And like a Christmas gift, I have no idea what I'll get when I uncover those cages and first peer in to say good morning. Today's gifts included;

Shock and Awe Snickerdoodle! His first reaction to seeing me was a great big *gasp!* and then the head twists of amazement, followed by "HUH?" The Big Doodle. The Doodle abides.

BuzzyBuzz Buzz Kirby. Perched on the edge of his hammock he peered up at me and spoke his truth of the day with a buzzy ham radio voice, "KirbyKirby. Good boy Kirby. Gimme a kiss." Cutest ham radio ever.

Chuckles the Butterbean. Butters being a girl known to conserve her energy on all matters simply looked out her door, and then at me. She quietly chuckles while inspecting her talons. I suppose a girl needs to take inventory for her day.

Parrots have telepathy. I know this because at this very moment there are three parrots growling at the window. They know FedEx is coming or, they are looking for trouble. Either way makes sense.

I may staple gun LeoBun's food bowl to the floor. He's dragging it everywhere and then up the ramp to throw it down the ramp. I understand he ate all his breakfast, this is painfully obvious. I understand he now suffers from the threat of the low blood sugars much like Felix, also painfully obvious. He throws himself on his side with a thud and a sigh. Over actor. There are no awards for over acting, rabbit. Except for Bugs Bunny. He got one.

2-3-17

I like to think of myself as the Landing Zone for all our aircraft.

Butters' lands on my head or shoulder like an albatross without a headwind. Big, bold and slightly startling. There's no reason to be startled of course, she announces her intentions with a mighty flock call of ignition. I know she's coming, and I know when she's landed. Her arrival feels like being shoved in the hallway back in grade school. Followed by a wet willie in the ear. Because she needs to let me know she's staying for a while.

Snickers' landing is far more subtle. You could say finessed with care. He only lands on my head and then rappels down to my shoulder. Snickers lands lightly like a helicopter. After the landing he continues to spin in a circle for a bit before going over the edge via my ear. His foot grip is so loose and light I have no idea how he doesn't over shoot the landing and just slide off and crash to the floor in a puddle of determined feathers.

Kirby is the jet fighter. Light and nimble and stealthy as a small blue ninja. I don't hear him coming, and I barely feel him land on my shoulder. It's almost as if he teleports. It's not so much a landing as it is a ShaZAM! He really needs a poof of smoke to finish the affect off.

Felix doesn't fly, therefor he doesn't land. The landing zone comes to him.

2-6-17

The bird room has an asphalt roof. It doesn't reflect the sun, but rather helps bake those in the room during the summer months. Dad spent Saturday and Sunday applying coats of bright white roof sealant to fix our reflection issues. His DIY became quite the game for Butters and Snickers.

A ladder leaning against the roof just outside a window is amazing and requires a good dressing down. Butters and Snickers growled, called out, and yelled at the ladder. They flew to the top of the macaw cage closest to the ladder window, warned said ladder they were watching it's every move and then burst into a flurry of jetted feathers around the house to land again in the same spot. There they leaned into the window and growled in sync. A menacing and ominous tone shared.

"rrrRRRAH!!"

I believe I saw that ladder quiver in fear.

When dad hauled up the leaf blower to, yes, blow leaves off the roof, the dangling bright orange wire was just the thing to refine the rules of engagement for Butters and Snickers.

Saturday was catch Dad coming down the ladder, catch Dad going up the ladder, follow dad's footsteps on the roof and yell at the ceiling, yell at the ladder, threaten the orange snake and fly in circles to yell at the ceiling some more day.

Sunday started slowly. This roof goop needs sun. It's winter in Florida, we start some days moist, dewy and chilly. So we all gathered in the bird room to share breakfast and time while the sun fought it's way through the winter atmosphere. Butters and Snickers were nonplussed and inpatient for the game to start.

Where's the ladder? Where's the snake? DAD! What are you still doing in here? They pouted and sat on their cages waiting for the game while we waited for the sun. 11:30 am and the sun announces it's arrival with illuminated palm trees and a brightened day.

I have never seen these two birds so excited as I did that Sunday at 11:38 am when Dad walked around the backyard with the ladder.

Right now, there are two macaws staring up and out windows looking for ladders and Dad, scrambling from cage top to cage top for a better view. Snickers is again, nonplussed, twisting his head robotically with a loud and uncertain "HUH?".

The roof is done Snickerdoodles. Please don't eat the house.

2-15-17

Kirby is going into a molt. This brings out Kirby Version 2.0. He needs to rub on everything, wants a bath every day, he's rather snarky, he's slightly impatient and antisocial if he doesn't want to be rubbed. Additionally, you have to rub against the grain of his feathers ever so lightly. Just enough to pull the feathers straight up so they fall back down with a little flip. Kirby snow storm of 2017 is predicted to be heavy with a chance of nippy. There is no preening him quite yet. That comes when his molt makes him look like a cat just spat him out.

This season he's discovered a roost behind our large post/beam in the dining room. He perches on the back of a guest chair, no one can see him there. Later in the day perching and removing loose feathers becomes necessary on Jamal-Pierre's side of the Piggles Condo.

Jamal-Pierre does not care. Werthers is ambivalent but seems to wonder why Kirby didn't bring some treats with him.

Felix is molting. There is no Felix Version 2.0. I'm sure if there was it would set my training back years.

I hand feed The Gambini Geckos. I like doing it so I know exactly who ate and how much. It's become obvious that my training is complete as they both laid out side by side and took worm turns during today's feeding. Donotelli is about 7 inches long now, so his teeth count for something. They are sharp little needles. I think he needs glasses, my fingers are not worms. Rotini can't be bothered to grab a worm. She just lays there with her mouth open and waits from me to insert her mealworms.

So. Trained. Am. I.

2-16-17

The Gambini Gecko Family come from a long line of Associates. Their family didn't do up the problems, they were the big-earners. So when Tony, Donotelli and Rottini landed in town most everybody knew they could get fingered.

Thing is, Tony didn't. Thing is, Donotelli already had the idea he needed to do up Tony to get where he needed to be with Rottini. But, I'm ahead of the story. Let's just say the Borgata was gonna get shook up sooner then later.

So Donotelli "Coffin Nail" Gambini, Tony "Eight Fingers" Gambini, and Rottini "The Eye" Camorra landed in town. You'd think a Gambini wouldn't be caught out with a Camorra but hey, Rottini was one of those girls that made things work. They don't call her "The Eye" for nothin.

Things went straight south quick the first night. Tony Eight Fingers wasn't eating. Donotelli Coffin Nail shrugged it off when Rottini wanted the answers. She liked Tony and wanted him around. Donotelli liked Rottini and didn't want Tony around. Donotelli was keep'n Tony on ice long enough to deal out that done. It wasn't a week before Donotelli "Coffin Nail" closed that hit. Tony "Eight Fingers" was no more, which is a thing you don't like mentioning. Offing family 'cause of things Hitt'n the Mattresses leaves a bad taste in your mouth. Like rotten mealworms.

And that's the story of Donotelli, Rottini and the late Tony. I suppose I could have just said we went to a local reptile breeder and chose three leopard geckos. I chose one very small weak looking one because I had hoped to save Tony's little life. But that's not turning a frown upside down.

2-17-17

How to Make a Kirby Lurker Bedtime Hammock;

Kirby likes to sleep in a hammock, and not so much in it as on the edge of it. Kirby likes to cling to the edge of things rather than perching. He's our little cliff diver. That's what he looks like when he launches off his varied cliffy favorite spots around the house. A little cliff diver with wings, he doesn't plummet down but catapults up and out and away.

I use jute or hemp in crochet. Be mindful of the smell of these products as some are produced with a treatment petroleum, why I have NO idea, but there it is. So give the spools a sniff, or if shopping online find those made outside China that use organic materials. Sorry China, but all your jute/hemp smells of lighter fluid.

I make a simple chain stitch 12-14 inches long, and then back again. Over and over until you hit about 4 inches width. I wash mine a few times in the machine to soften up the fibers and remove any loose debris and dirt.

How you attach it is up to you. There's all kinds of options from simply leaving enough corner string to tie, to C locks to clips to whatever. The goal as always is safety for our sleeper.

I'm going to sew a hammock out of felt with thicker folded edges and see what he thinks of that version. Maybe a matching pillow. May as well go overboard while I'm here.

2-21-17

Blue Jays are jerks. Shady jerks that can't be trusted. According to Butters, Blue Jays are shady jerks that can't be trusted and are as worthless as turtles that can't think around corners. She's made it pretty clear that I need to get a net and go get these scoundrels out of her backyard trees NOW.

She finds one particular Blue Jay, we'll call him Dean, totally uncouth. Dean has a very impressive mimic of a whistle I've never heard before Dean, but Butters seems to identify it as a direct insult to her lineage.

Her tactic is simple; sit on top of the open door of her cage, lean toward the window with half open wings, pinned eyes and a wide WIDE open beak yelling "SNICKERS! BLAH!"

I taught Snickers and Butters "Blah" as a way to let me know when things aren't working for them. Dean is not working for Butters. Snickers keeps raising his head and looking at Butters with every anti-Dean Holler asking "HUH? WHAT?" Snickers and Butters are starting to act like a married couple.

LeoBun is digging to China. He picked a spot in his condo and found the perfect corner to crack his linoleum floor. I heard the new rabbit excavation sound and ran into the dining room to see his new project. China has enough issues, they do not need an excavating LeoBun popping up in the middle of Beijing. Leo's look of, "Step back, this is a secure site." was message enough. I ran upstairs fast to get a wooden insert meant for dividing the condo to cover his digging site. He was working furiously and I was running like there was a rabbit eating linoleum in my house.

The extra bits for the condo are in the companion animal extra bits and pieces of stuff, closet. In other words I have to excavate, too. I find the prized perfectly sized wood slat and turn to run back, my big toe catches a metal rod extra bit from building the piggles condo and wham, the metal rod falls on my other big toe. I used words I've learned for when things aren't working for me.

At this moment there's a rabbit sitting on top of a wood slat that is blocking his work. Have you ever seen that Discovery Channel video where there's a fox jumping straight up and then diving into deep snow to route out a rabbit? That's LeoBun. I guess if you can't dig, you blast your way to Beijing.

2-27-17

Cali's home sick. Poor guy. He's suffering downstairs with the flock in the bird room. Felix is asleep on his digesting perch I'm sure. It is 3:36 in the afternoon and he should have polished off his after lunch before dinner snack, snack.

I can hear Butters singing "peekaboo!" Snickers is ringing his bell and growling "RAWR!" Kirby is onto his afternoon repertoire, "Good boy Kirby. chirpachirp chirpachirp, you are a good boy kirbykirby. BruiserBee! Come here. Step up. Gimme a kiss. Hey buddy. What are you doin? Chirpachirpa CHIRP!" The four members of the Horde are whistling loud and proud into their window.

Cali coughs a lung clearing hack and this sends two macaws into fake sneezing and one napping African Grey into an impressive set of fake coughs.

I have no idea how Cali can even hear the gun battle on Xbox at all.

Where am I? Upstairs on the laptop writing. I noticed this is the only room in the whole house that isn't scented with bird. I do smell all the creative smells of papers, paints, charcoals, cloth and fiber and clay and wood. It's hard to get started and focused on one thing up here. I could do anything and everything is within reach. It's difficult to choose what happy I prefer. And after I choose I can see what I did not choose out of the corner of my eye.

This must be what a parrot feels like all the time.

3-1-17

It's wash day for the furry ones. Time to disinfect cages and give piggles a bath. And one small dog, too. It's also mop the floors week, but that's the main event for another day.

This all gets tricky with success and ease depending on the dactyls behaving. So you know, it's sketchy at best. Snickers likes hanging on the child gate we use to cut off the fast through pass through window into the kitchen. He also likes watching me bath piggles and one small dog. He is waiting for the wet towels I use to dry them. He really likes fussing over fresh wet towels. It's his thing.

Did I mention Kirby has a day cage now? He confiscated Felix's RV cage for his own day cage. It sits on the dining table in the Piggle'n Bun Cafe. It's his favorite place during the day. Today it was a holding pen for piggles. Kirby didn't care, he likes his piggles. I put a piggles in the pen, clean their side of the condo. Take that piggles and bathe that piggles and dry that piggles and put him back in his newly cleaned side. All the while Kirby is on my shoulder assisting. He's looking for spots I may miss.

Two piggles and two piggle condo sides done. Snickers is now in his unlocked cage on the bottom towels playing with damp post piggle bath towels. Growls, and chuckles galore. Butters is napping on the door of her cage. She can't be bothered with all this business. Felix is digesting on his perch after feasting on feasts on the third step up of the staircase.

Dactyls securely busy it's time to move the LeoBun so that I can clean his cage. I could take him upstairs to his play room, but as of late, he is less than impressed. He just prefers the condo. I scoop him up, kiss his nose and put him up in the second floor of his condo with all his favorite toys and a few treats. There's a divider door where the top of his ramp meets that floor. I have securely closed that. He's upstairs, I'm working on his downstairs.

Scrubbing away half my body squirmed into the cage I hear Felix yell, "STOP!" then a whistle and the Anti-Snickers Bell Alarm. I yank my body out of the condo opening and rush in to find Snickers still on his cage floor towels, but under the damp towels. I can't even see him. Felix just wanted to get his attention.

And mine. "Seriously Fee, I've got work to do." Fartsound Chuckle is his response.

I return to the piggle and bunny dining area to finish the LeoBun Condo makeover only to find LeoBun throwing all his toys that were upstairs, now downstairs, out of the door I am using for access. Clunk, donk, dunk bink, and bonk. He looks at me. I can hear Cartman's voice in my head, "I do what I want."

Duly note there is securely closed, and then there is securely bunny closed. I did not execute the latter. In this house you generally get to keep what you kill. In other words, you figure out how to open a door to come down, you get to stay down. Turns out LeoBun is a pretty good assistant on cleaning day.

If you call throwing towels, toys, food bowls and bedding out the same door I'm using to stick myself into, helping. Most rabbits would I think.

3-2-17

The itsy bitsy spider went up the bonsai tree. And created a few hundred itsier-bitsier babies.

My favorite spider is the Kite Spider. They are small, armored in brilliant geometry and colors and relentless. I like all that in a little spider. My 7 foot specimen bonsai tree is a Kite Spider nursery this year. I lost count as to the to number of family members but I never loose interest in visiting them and watching them weave their webs.

I accidentally drove my hatted head into one of the webs over the weekend. I had a gardening hat on with a wide brim, it took out a portion of one junior spider's web while I watered my tree. I felt the strength and tactile pull of his web on my brim and immediately regretted my carelessness. After all, I'm in his neighborhood, I should have better manners.

Junior didn't care. He just hooked 4 new anchor lines from fence to tree branches and made due with his new center point. Junior just didn't care. He simply continued to spider.

I like that about little spiders.

Today is clean the tops of ceiling fans day. Also known as, "WOW! There's alot of cockatiel poop up here!"

Today is also spot clean the drop zone areas around cages day. We try to keep towels placed under the resting/perching areas so the dactyls do their do on towels rather than floors. But alas, Bruiser our senior dementia dog snarfs around all the towels looking for parrot leftovers and the towels are left in lumps and piles in the wrong spots. Then Turner, the smaller dementia senior, pees on them.

It gets weird around here.

Tomorrow is mop day and take a few cages outside to hose down day. I probably won't sleep tonight for the excitement of it.

3-5-17

One speech is written. One is started. 2000 more words to my second book. A sketching laid out in hard pencil for a piece due in July and three parrot consults closed out. I sit in my studio perplexed as to what to do next.

Kirby sits on my shoulder buzzing like a radio making the most brilliant suggestion.

And so we work mindlessly and mindfully on a Minion puzzle. The three boys are on the beach with surfboards and blowups. Strangely enough, there is no banana. Minion on a beach is just what my studio wall needs.

Kirby has the best ideas.

3-7-17

I pulled the cover back from Butters' bedroom roost, her eye lit up and she said hello with Buttery sincerity. I opened her cage door so she, like Snickers and Kirby, could come out to perch on the door and wake up for a new day.

Instead she raised her left foot and said hello again. I gave her my left pointer finger to grab. Her foot is warm and strong, and she smells like sunshine. Butters started bobbing her head and eventually used the back of my hand as a bongo. Tapping her beak on me and purring. Sunshine and macaw purrs. I am a lucky girl.

Meanwhile, Snickers is in the shower executing HazMat Evac Procedures. That boy does not "bird" until he's done that. No way. I don't own a mop big enough.

Kirby is busy speaking to the bathroom mirror letting himself know he is a very good boy and his name is Kirby. I realize I've done that for myself at times.

Felix is downstairs laser beaming loudly with a sonar ping for good measure. He is worried I'll forget to come back downstairs.

The Horde are busy eating leafy greens and parsley. My location is now irrelevant.

LeoBun is playing soccer with his big grass ball. It's bigger than his head by two times. He loves that thing. He knows I'll be back around noon and continues kicking his ball back and forth without a care in his bunny world.

Werthers and Jamal-Pierre are both in food comas. They don't come out of that until roughly 11:45 or when I open the fridge.

I am where I am supposed to be, and was where I was supposed to be earlier.

3-9-17

I don't get out much, on purpose, under my own directive. Everybody knows that I am a reclusive unicorn. But I went out today. I went to the dry cleaners. The owner is hilarious. I love her and have known her since the first day of kickboxing and martial arts. She hemmed my karategi pants and blouse sleeves. It's really hard to get a 5' 6" girly shaped karategi. Kid you not. You have to be willing to aftermarket.

She made me laugh today when I dropped off a pile of clothes with history. Our personal inside joke; it will take a year for me to remember to pick all this up.

Stopped at Office Depot for printer ink. Um. NO, Office Depot. Have you heard of the internets? You can shop there and get better prices with no sales tax or shipping costs. It is really cool. You should look into it, because your prices are confused. I walked out of Office Depot with no printer ink.

I arted at Michael's, which I can't write about because my Mom and Dad read my Muses.

Popped into Target, the French Riviera Walmart, for toothpaste and sticky hooks. I bought Tom's toothpaste. Because I am weird about Fluoride. Fluoride is the government's way to insert nanobots into your bloodstream and control your thoughts and record your conversations. I bought sticky hooks because Snickers can't leave the pull-strings for the horizontal blinds alone while sitting in the window yelling at whatever it is that is annoying his view. He has to try and grab them with his tongue and a sneaky lean. Well the joke's on you and your sneaky lean tongue Snickerdoodles! I am raising the hooks so you and your sneaky tongue can't reach them. Neener!

My final parking job was executed at Publix Grocery. I want everyone to know that doesn't have access to a Publix Grocery that I sincerely am sorry for that fact. Publix is a Florida bragging right. I grabbed the few missing elements to get the flock, my husband and I through to the weekend. And beer. I bought beer. Hurray beer!

All the while I am texting with my BFF, Felix's Vet, and super female friend Nichole. She is also hilarious. And super smart. We are doing lunch tomorrow to talk about arting her house. We send laughing emojis and hearts at the end of our conversation. So BFF.

So here I am, home, stuff unpacked and put away and I am listening to Snickerdoodles sing while making up songs like a really bad opera singer. He is teaching Butters, I Love YOOOUUU!!! This is new. I always thought it odd, of all the things I say multiple times a day, I love you is said the most. You'd think someone would be up on that.

I guess my love just needed a melody.

3-14-17

As of 2:45 pm today, I have applied the phrase, "Snickers! I'm watching you! Be a good boy!" 19 times. Snickers has responded with, "Snickerdoodles is a good boy!" 7 times.

The remaining 12 times include crashing toys, opera singing, hanging upside down by one talon growling "BLAH!", throwing noodles on the dog, running across the floor with a stainless steel bowl, throwing said bowl then grabbing said bowl to clamor up the side of the domed cage so he can pound the bowl on the top of the dome. Clamoring down the cage to run across the floor to get to my feet, lift a foot and invitingly inquire, "HUH?"

I have two halves of each morning. Pre-Dactyl and Post-Dactyl. Pre-Dactyl it's me, 2 piggles, 1 bun, 1 Felix and for today, the soft push of the heater as it warms the house from last night's Florida cold snap. I type, create and make a list as to what I need to accomplish during the next 10 hours.

Post-Dactyl it's all the aforementioned, 2 Dactyls, 1 Kirby, and me throwing out my newly formulated to do list. Adding 2 Dactyls to a recipe is equivalent to adding nitroglycerine to your little red wagon, as you pull it up hill, on a gravel road, on square wheels, blindfolded.

It all looked good on paper earlier.

3-20-17

The house smells like Florida Spring, and the songs of all our shore and song birds are filling the house. I opened the front windows of the house first thing today. I love song bird music. The sun won't be on the front of the house for a while, so the air is cool, a bit humid, and fresh.

Butters is on my shoulder looking out the open window. She smells like sunshine. Open windows just push her button of joy and release this Essence de beurres. That's what I'm naming this fragrance if I figure out how to bottle it.

Snickers doesn't trust the open window. It's all fishy to him. He's jumping back and forth between macaw cages in the bird room, pretending not to look out the front window.

He has the window totally fooled.

The Horde's window is wide open, they are preening and falling into naps. In one hour the mail person will walk by talking on her cellphone and totally gatecrash their Zen. They really do not like her walk-bys much. She's loud, and the conversations are generally high school level gossip. I have to ask myself, WHY do I know she has a friend who is pregnant? Why do I know she doesn't think that friend is capable of taking care of herself, let alone a baby?

I'll probably close the windows before she shows up. Neither I, nor the Horde enjoy her walk-bys now that I think about it.

Kirby is asleep in his Kirby Condo. He has completely adopted Felix's RV to the point of needing it for his daily lifestyle moments. I'll have to get another Felix RV, for Felix.

3-22-17

It is not possible to prove to a piggles that he is sitting on his breakfast. One must serve a second breakfast at a location far from the first breakfast to get the piggles to get off his breakfast that he does not believe exists.

3-23-17

There are two woodpeckers working the Oak tree directly in front of the Horde's window. I've got the window open again to let the morning cool come in for a while.

At first the Horde as a whole were totally unimpressed with a woodpecker's idea of foraging. With every rat-a-tat-tat they would flutter and fly and scream at the window. Until Winston decided to have a dance off.

Oh, it's ON.

Now the woodpeckers face a determined male cockatiel. He answers every rat-a-tat-tat with his own against his mirror.

Woodpeckers, you just got served.

Felix fartsounded to make sure the woodpeckers understood just how served they got.

I haven't quite figured it out yet, but Snickers has decided hanging upside down on the bathroom door frame before going morning HazMat Controlled Poop is mandatory. This is now a thing.

If I end up in a nursing home when I'm old, I'm going to do the same thing every morning. That'll give the CNAs something to think about.

3-24-17

I've got first floor mopping down to a science. The Dactyls stay out of their cages for their favorite spectator sport; Watching Mom Mop. Snickers has gotten so very good these last 6 months. He's just a really good boy. Butters has always been that dream dactyl. Behaved, kind, loving, quiet. So now the audience is fully agreeable.

Grapes are in their bowls today. Red grapes. Cold from the refrigerator's fruit drawer. This is the sport snack of choice this Friday. While I work on the last 10% of the first floor, Snickers is sucking on a grape on the door of his cage, as I mop directly in front of him.

"HUH?" He's concerned for my energy level obviously.

"I'm good Snickers. Thanks for asking. How's your grape?" I mop under the door and around.

"MMMmm!" The grape is now a soggy red skin hanging from his tongue as he confirms the excellence of the experience, and drops it directly on the spot I just mopped.

Hooligan.

It's really hard to put furniture back where it belongs after mopping. All the poop outlines are gone.

3-24-17

According to Audubon.org the Roseate Spoonbill is:

"Gorgeous at a distance and bizarre up close is the Roseate Spoonbill. Locally common in coastal Florida, Texas, and southwest Louisiana, they are usually in small flocks, often associating with other waders. Spoonbills feed in shallow waters, walking forward slowly while they swing their heads from side to side, sifting the muck with their wide flat bills."

According to Butters the Roseate Spoonbill is; a pink untrustworthy trespassing menace that better get that slow walking swinging head OUT OF HER BACKYARD RIGHT NOW!!!

3-28-17

The dogs are slowly aging to crazy. I say this with love. Dementia and getting old isn't funny, and yet we are all heading in that direction and quite frankly I tend to laugh at inappropriate times. Ask my mom about Church services when I was single digit age. Father Hettinger never made it past the third kneeling prayer without my sisters and I sniggering with our foreheads resting on our little clasped hands, faces hidden behind the pew in knelt prayer. And honestly I have NO idea what was funny. But there we knelt sniggering through Catholic blessings every Sunday morning, or Saturday night if Dad had to mow the lawn on Sunday. So yes, I don't necessarily need a correct reason to laugh. Anyway...

As of late Bruiser and Turner have been holding Gladiator Events around 5 am. Not every morning, but when it suits their lust for battle. Best I can tell Turner gets tired of Bruiser mindlessly wandering in circles around the house. He just hits a point where he wants Bruiser to lay down. Bruiser has advanced Cushing's Disease, so he pants like a steam engine while he's wandering aimlessly and mindlessly and infinitely around the house.

Turner can't take that.

So best I can tell, and having witnessed during their Matinee Gladiator Events, Turner launches himself from a sleeping spot right into Bruisers head. Mind you, Turner has no teeth. He's just gumming Bruiser into submission. He delivers the epic terrier growls of death and attacks blindly.

Bruiser takes it for a few minutes and then retaliates with a bark/whine and stepping on Turner's head.

No one dies. No one is injured and no one asks me for a thumbs up or thumbs down at these events. It's really lousy Gladiatoring.

During the 5 am shows, I just lay in bed and listen to the short, unimpressive battle of demented wills come to a close with both competitors going back to their geriatric therapeutic mattressed corners.

I hear heavy sighs, and old dog tongues smacking as they try to get their drool under control. Then I hear LeoBun thump 3 or 4 no nonsense foot stomps letting them both know he has had quite enough of all that pointless dog business.

Night before last I was forced to come downstairs to break up a battle that had gone on a bit too long, and had gotten a bit too loud. Bruiser had found his inner warrior. I rather felt like Julius Caesar descending the stairs in judgment. Who would I find under who's sword? Would the crowds demand death or pity for the conquered? Would a Gladiator Soul find it's way to the god's this day?

None of the above. I found two old dogs sitting straight up, leaning against each other panting, drooling and working really hard at looking like nothing was going on. Two sets of eyes with the "Who me?" message.

They really are lousy Gladiators.

3-29-17

According to my calendar, today is when I start really thinking about what I am going to wear up to Lehigh Valley Bird Expo to speak. I'm keynote, so I suppose I need to dress to impress. I speak twice, opening and closing sessions, so I need to dress comfortably. I'll be up there 3 nights and 3 days so I need to make sure I pack stuff that's comfortable and fits in a backpack that I can shove under the seat on the plane because I am not checking bags. Nor am I trying to fit something up in the luggage stowage area, because trying to fit a larger carry on up there is a drag while bumping into other people who are also bummed about trying.

As I stand in the walk-in, looking at my wardrobe I realize two important facts that I'll need to deal with; One, I don't care about clothes, or shoes or wardrobes. Two, I own a wardrobe that is 60% companion modified. I've got 30 day's to overcome these speed bumps of fashion. Worst case scenario I show up in the latest Bird Lady Look for 2017. Which is me, in jeans, and a Because Parrot T-Shirt holding a muffin from the breakfast buffet at the hotel. There may or may not be bird poop on my back.

Kirby has been my fashion assistant while I mull all this over. He jumped from my shoulder onto a hanger and is now playing monkey gymnastics between hangers. Climbing in and out of my shirts, jumping between hangers and rod, and it seems he's counting buttons. This is why I won't know if there is poop on my back when I'm up at LeHigh.

Snickers is climbing into the dry cleaning basket. He needs to throw everything out of it. I already did that preemptively and replaced everything with parrot towels. Basically I had to swap out the dry cleaning basket with clean towels and hide the dry cleaning from Kirby because of the buttons before I could stare at a very limited wardrobe.

I'm watching Kirby Gymnastics and Snickers Nesting.

This is why I don't have a wardrobe.

Butters flys to the top of the door of the master bedroom and succinctly poops down the back of the door and on the door handle. I know this not because I hear it, but because I hear her say, "Oh!" That Oh only goes with pooping. Call it the Garanimals of parrot communication. They match perfectly.

Felix is downstairs half asleep on his tent looking out the open window. His only concern; will the neighbor use that hose in his direction.

The Horde look out the other open window without cares of any kind. That tends to be the way of the Horde. Unless the mail lady approaches.

3-29-17

I am part terrier. I'm far happier jumping from one shiny to another and back again. I complete more projects when there are more than one project. I really like shiny new ideas, and if they are really disco, then it's on like Donkey Kong.

I'm currently fostering Grenadine. I named her Grenadine. I believe all guitars should be named. Grenadine's owner couldn't take her along his journey, so he left her with me. Of course as with any good fostering, you take your new foster for a checkup. I took Grenadine to Seven C Music and Joel gave her a thorough refresh and once over.

I love Grenadine. I hope in the long run, I am a Foster Failure. I have another guitar, a gift from my husband, Lara. She's not going anywhere. She needs her checkup refresh, but I don't want to give her up just yet. She's a gift, so you can see how I don't want to let her go.

I am also fostering an amp that is Grenadine's companion. Yes, I had to sew an amp cover that matches both of them. I play the piano. I don't play the guitar. Yet.

They are so shiny.

3-30-17

Summer's creeping into Florida. Morning dew points are leaving the boat wet and slick, dripping itself dry in the rising sun. I can't leave the front windows open much longer, it's 68 degrees and barely a cool breeze. But I love the sound of song and shore birds. I'll hang on a little longer for today.

A long time ago, on a vacation at Hilton Head I stood out on a patio overlooking the ocean. A morning coffee in my hand I would just sip and smell the salty air quietly. The kids were still asleep, and the other tourists hadn't hit the beach yet. The mix of that coffee smell and ocean hooked me for life. It took 20 years to get here properly. And today I stood on my back porch watching the egrets in the creek, hearing seagull complaining off in the distance. And in my hand was coffee bringing that smell and mixing in with the humid salty air. I was almost back where my heart first yearned for all this...how perfect a moment to stand in gratitude surrounded by these sounds and sites and smells.

On another note, I looked in the mirror and realized I had slept in a shirt that had Kirby poop trailing down the front of it.

Nice.

4-3-17

Once upon a time I was 10 going on 11. I was also a victim of ageism. Certainly I had the air of a teenager. I most certainly had the humor and intellect of a freshman in college.

And yet, the library lady wouldn't let me come up the stairs to the adult section of the library. Mendota's library is in a magnificent stone building. It's legacy looms in the center of the park. There's a stone water fountain you can drink from before going in. When you take a sip you have to hold a handle down with the palm of your hand and then stand tippy toe on the top stones to drink. The wet stones smell old, and the water tastes like cold water filtered through river rock. The park is filled with old maple trees. They are as old as the library and carry their own legacy.

If you were a victim of ageism, you couldn't walk up the front stone steps to pull on the heavy lead glass doors to go in. That was for adults only. You had to follow a sidewalk to the right and walk down steps to the basement and children's library. When you first walked in the side door you faced the reality of ageism if you were 10 going on 11 with the air of a teenager and the humor and intellect of a freshman in college. There were steps to the left going up to the real books, and the steps to the right going down to the fake books.

And that's how I saw it. The books downstairs weren't the real ones. They were full of pictures and honestly didn't tell you anything you couldn't figure out on your own. It was upstairs where the real stories and the real words lived.

I snuck up there one afternoon when the librarian was busy at her desk helping an adult I recognized. He knew my dad. Dad knew him and they talked about woodworking in the driveway sometimes.

I took that last step up the stairs into the adult library, and scurried to the right, out of sight. I could smell the real books. Oh yes, they were musty and warm and full of words I wanted to read. I stood in one room where the windows went from floor to domed ceiling. And was immediately found out by the not busy now librarian.

I think on all this today because I just bought an eBook at Amazon.

It was too easy, there was no adventure. It sits in digital black and white on my cellphone inside a digital library named Kindle. The words are there for my taking and yet I feel I cheated the system, or the intended beauty of searching for "that book".

4-4-17

Butters is so very happy right now. My hair has grown out since the Long Island Expo in October. It's back to a rich shade of brown, and it's long enough to be pulled back in a hair twistie again. Which means hair twistie pull offs are available! She's on my head right now laughing with a twistie in her beak, while I struggle to see the monitor through all the hair hanging in my face.

The turtle population coming out of the creek has increased 3 fold the last week. They meander round and round and round the field behind our yard. Somehow they are operating on a shared GPS signal. They are all staying in front of Butters' window. I'm practicing my speeches while she's setting off Anti-Turtle Dactyl Alarms. The alarms are winning. I can't hear a word I'm saying.

Although I think I sound pretty good. At least it feels like my lips are forming real words in the right order.

Snickers is going into a light molt. He's the last one in the clan this season. He tends to hang onto them for an hour or so after he pulls them out. Carefully inspecting his fallen feather, chewing the hard tip and making sure there is nothing else he can get out of it that may be useful. He is frugal with his feathers.

LeoBun is heading into a coat blow. I'm brushing him 3 times a day to stay ahead of the coming tsunami of fur. You know your Bun has an attitude when he rings a service bell for a 4th brushing. He just stands in front of his door, shaking his ball bell. I open the door to explain the conflict of my schedule and his demands and he throws his empty food dish out the door.

Well EXCUSE ME rabbit.

Or course I put a few treats in the bowl, place the bowl back and begin spa treatment number 4. I'm not a barbarian. Buns have needs.

4-4-17

Godzilla Turtle just came out of the creek. She's a softshell turtle. She's massive. I had to walk out there to believe her size. She's twice as wide as Edgar (our largest local crow) is big. She's digging in the soft sand base near the creek edge, experimenting to find the perfect spot for egg laying. The crows are following behind her as she turns soil over. They are feasting on grubs and bugs.

Godzilla Turtle doesn't care about any of the it. She is large and in charge and Butters about passed out when she crawled out of the creek.

In fact, right now Godzilla Turtle is so close and so massive and so doesn't care, Butters isn't sounding the Anti-Turtle Dactyl Alarm. She is just perched stiff as a board growl whining.

Unimpressed with her fear factor, Felix just fart sounded and turned his back to her.

Living the Successful Companion Parrot Lifestyle is not living in a vacuum. Everything we take out into the world from our companion life reverbs back to us and our birds. We aren't crazy bird people. We are lucky people who get to share their world with an emotional, cognitive, choice making friend with feathers.

You can't have a successful flock, if you, personally, are not having a successful sincere life. I bring this up because this morning I'm running late on posts due to a couple flocks under stress and feeling a bit lost. They thought their birds were acting out, but in reality, they were reacting out. Wasting their precious time on the wrong problems.

Parrots are not complicated. They are simply yes or no. WE are the complicated piece of the equation. Be a parrot. Life is just life. Sometimes we like it, sometimes we don't. But it's the only one we have, so you better make a mess, get loud, eat with joy, play with sincerity and never leave a room without a good loud flock call.

In the last 15 minutes I've said the following out loud;

You are not eating that walnut on my head.

Don't eat the house.

Don't eat the door.

What are you doing on the floor, chasing the dog, dragging that towel?

Heyyy HEY! You on the TV. Get off the TV.

and, Heyyy HEY! That's a staircase, not your monkey bars, monkey.

I've only been talking to one bird.

LeoBun has a new litter box. It's one of those compressed recycled paper ones. He's really busy in there trying to chew it all into the shape he likes for laying in it. He's pretty precise with his lounge sculpting.

Snickers is convinced these are not rabbit construction sounds bouncing through the house, but rather, Dad. Dad is doing something somewhere in this house!

Dad. Where is Dad?

He's walking around the floor calling for him. He's flying from cage to cage to tree stand flock calling louder.

I've shown him Leo working. I've let him see and listen to the BunCondo Construction. Nope.

Dad is here. I am a fraud. There is no rabbit.

4-14-17

Kirby has never tried or eaten an in the shell Pistachio. Felix and I are currently sharing squash and pumpkin seeds. And pistachios on the side for Felix.

Kirby flies over, raids the pistachio bag and obliterates 3 in the shell pistachios like a boss. My desk is dusted with the remains of collateral damages.

I hope there isn't any turf wars in the future around here.

4-19-17

Bruiser, our old man golden retriever, is still inspired to chase a squirrel. Well, not chase, more like lean forward with a good memory of a chase from the past.

This morning I found myself reminding him not to chase the pregnant squirrels. Which is silly, the girls were reaching under him to grab their breakfast bits. He was just standing over their breakfast pile gazing off into the distance thinking on the past. Not a care in the world or a concern for the 6 pregnant squirrels scurrying under and around him.

One girl grabbed an orange piece he was standing on. I think she even said, "excuse me old man".

Kirby's last new feather has finally grown in. His tail is complete. He is 100% upgraded for this molting season. And let me tell you he sounds like a helicopter on his flight missions.

Felix is slightly honked at me for yesterday. Butters let me know this morning she wasn't going near her cage, and she is keeping a close eye on all my intentions. She's had quite enough of being in a cage. Snickers doesn't care, he's got things to get into, and he really doesn't care where the things are as long as he can get into them.

I'll be spending the day utilizing my "no one is going in a cage" body language. Felix has asked me three times already, "Time to go bye bye?"

No Fee, it's time to make sure your foods bowls don't disappoint you all day long.

4-21-17

It's 3-ish. Felix is to my right on his tent. Asleep. Kirby is cleaning his toes buzzing happily to my left on the top shelf. Butters is inside Felix's cage sleepy growling. (if you've a BG Macaw, you know this sound). Snickers is inside his cage on his grooming perch with his bell and dangle toys hanging on his back, asleep. The Horde is allopreening and trying not to fall asleep.

Snickers is in his cage because I was vacuuming which made him loose his birdy brain which caused an insane need to fly around trying to get into every water bowl available to bath which is fine if it's not Felix's water bowl, which is the water bowls he was adamant about.

I gotta vacuum!

So in he goes with 3 little metal cups and a big bowl of water. I lay down 3 towels to sop up the coming tsunami and go back to vacuuming.

But I digress. Everyone is napping(ish). IF I stop typing and walk upstairs to shower, this current circuit of flockery breaks.

I gotta shower!

Conundrum indeed.

4-24-17

Best laid plans...

I was going to clean piggles condo and sweep the floor in the Piggles'n Bun Cafe. But Bun is asleep, on his side, with one ear wrapped around his face held by one bunny foot. His nose is twitchy and happy. I can't even.

I was going to replace the teeny teeny, TEENY tiny, screw in my computer glasses so I can wear them like a normal person, but I can't see with my progressive glasses to fix my seeing eyeball pair of glasses. I was so smart for like, 3 minutes.

I was going to do laundry. I shared pasta with parrots instead.

I was going to run through my two speeches. I practiced guitar instead. I'm sure I'll make some sort of sense up north, if all else fails I'll break out in a guitar solo.

I was going to accomplish so much adulting, then new Lego people came in the mail.

I'm so off the rails I've decided to just make that the new plan.

Off the rails. Winning!

4-28-17

I finished a 30 minute Qi Gong meditation with a Scarlet Macaw on my head. I started my 30 minute Qi Gong meditation with a blue and gold macaw on my head. I have no idea if this qualifies as meditation.

I practiced guitar for 30 minutes on Lara and 30 minutes on Dorothy with 2 macaws perched in a tree together singing along for 50 minutes. I'm starting a band. Dactyl Harmonics.

My sister called. We talked for about 15 minutes and laughed and laughed. This is way better than meditations.

I folded parrot towels for 5 minutes. Snickers threw all those folded towels on the floor in 30 seconds. Who's smarter?

No matter what, we invest time, save time or waste time. I prefer investing. It pays off big.

Invest wisely.

5-1-17

Snickers just started singing, "I Love you!" This is the second time he's worked these words out loud. Butters is now trying to join in.

I will hug two macaws before I type another word. I'm melting right into the floor from all this radioactive cute.

5-3-17

Tomorrow I fly out to PA. This is the hard part of what I do personally. Leaving all that I adore to do what I am passionate about for a few days. A few days is a lifetime. I miss my husband, I miss the flock, I miss piggles n buns n lizards n dogs. I suppose I might be whining a bit. I'm not sure. Dad will be here the whole time. Felix will be in charge of his four day SaturDADday. My head knows they will flourish, my heart says, "Who can survive without ME!?"

A girlfriend came over today. Which was a fabulous moment in time. She brought big gifts for dactyls. Dactyls are currently avoiding the new toys in their cages because OBVIOUSLY I am trying to trap them. Silly Dactyls.

Butters and Kirby have been swapping my shoulders all day long. Kirby wants left. Butters wants right. Neither get that they could share me at the same time. I'm like an unsuccessful Timeshare in Cancun.

Snickers is growling at a moth flying around his head. He is a total bad to the bone boy. That moth has no idea.

5-12-17

On the couch feeling sick, playing with my new Google phone. Nurse Lurker is keeping an eye on me. Felix obviously has no interest in either point.

5-17-17

Life is self-leveling. It is also Ninja Dodgeball. You can't see things coming sometimes, but if you take the hit and allow that short moment of shock to ebb and flow as it should, it'll all self-level.

Kirby inherited a water bowl. Known now as the Kirby Soaking Tub.

LeoBun has inherited a first floor. Cali is making him a ramp, so that he can come out and run around for playtime with me.

I inherited towels that no longer move or get wadded up, thereby staying where I laid them, to whit, less parrot poop on wood floors.

Snickers inherited a tree stand that no longer gets surfed on. Which is easier than perching on a tree stand surf board.

Cali and I inherited a floor that collects dropped parrot food rather than becoming a buffet table OF dropped parrot food. Now he and I REALLY know how much is hitting the floor rather than bird crops. I am currently ignoring this newly revealed information.

I inherited new jewelry. I wear Turner's collar as a bracelet because the jingle sound the tag makes will always make me smile.

New norms are appearing every day. We are self-leveling. Sad thoughts are beginning to back fill with happy memories.

Bruiser ate alot of dropped parrot food! He should have been the size of a new born beluga whale.

Saying goodbye to our companion dogs after 15 and some years left a hole wide as the sea. Every day a small memory comes back and falls into that hole. We are self-leveling.

5-17-17

Snickers is on top of the dome cage, romancing one of his girlfriends. He keeps saying, "stop" "stopit" "oh!".

She must be the kinky one.

5-22-17

Last Thursday, I was cohabiting with Flu and could only lay on the couch and think-write. I did quite a bit of think-writing these past few days with Flu. It was the kind of flu that knocks you off your feet on Day 1. Day 2 you think you feel better until you stand up and Flu laughs at you, in your own head, and throws you back down on the couch. Day 3 Flu lets you think you are hungry until you look at food and then you remember you can't think or look at food. Flu is a jerk.

The upside of Flu is the care I received through Parrot HealthCare Services. Felix was Floor Director. His job was simple; keep the One Eye on things. Snickers and Butters were Observational Nurses. I was given vast quantities of overlookings and woke up once covered in stuffed toys. It seems Snickers felt it necessary to take all his stuffed toys, mini blankets, girlfriends, and tennis balls off the top of his cage and drop them on me. I napped through that procedure.

Kirby lurkered next to me and on me the entire time. I'm pretty sure he was applying holistic healing massage therapy as he continually walked up and down the length of my body stopping at my head every once in a while to take my temperature with his tongue via my ear canal.

I'm really glad human doctors don't do that.

5-23-17

My computer mouse feels like an off road vehicle on a gravel road right now. Kirby is eating a pellet above my mouse pad.

"Snickers. Don't water board your girlfriend. That's not nice."
(So he gets the other girlfriend and dunks her in the other water bowl. Obviously my instructions weren't clear.)

"Felix, seriously dude, quit antagonizing Snickers." (*fartsound doorknock fartsound* Lip from a grey.)

"Butterbean! Relax, it's just four crows. They need to eat, too!" (She hops to the other cage top to scream louder at a different angle.)

"Can you eat that popcorn somewhere else other than my head, Kirby?" (Nope.)

"Bun! Look at you running up and down your BunRamp!" (At which time my exuberant mom mode sends him straight up the ramp to the second floor of his condo.)

For every reaction there is an equal and opposite action around here. It's almost science.

5-31-17

The cautious journey of a Bun and his ramp. One does not simply bunny hop down a randomly new ramp! This is not the Way of the Bun.

Day 1 of the Way of the Bun. Ignore said random ramp.

Day 2 of the Way of the Bun. SlowMo Bunny Hops down halfway. This is followed by the Bunny Alertness Stare of Doom. Because obviously we built a ramp that leads to doom. QUICK! Run back up the ramp and under the towel tent! This is followed by Bun Stares of Doom from under the towel tent, at the randomly new ramp heading toward doom.

Day 3 of the Way of the Bun. Throw your breakfast greens onto the ramp along with the left over apple slice as offerings to the Bun Gods for safe travels.

At least that's what I think that was all about. I could be wrong.

6-1-17

You can get up in the morning and think you have a plan. It is something available to all humans.

79

You can get up and start your day with the plan laid out before your brain like the yellow brick road. You, Dorothy, or Scarecrow if you're a dude, are ready to skip all the way through to the end. You got this.

THEN. Life wakes up a nano second after you and laughs and laughs and laughs as it rolls out of bed right behind you. Life knows better. Life is about to jack your plans up.

Go ahead and brush your teeth confidently. This will not help.
Sure, brush your hair. This will not help.
Get dressed. This will not help.
Drink coffee. This will not help.
Act normal. That never helps.

Because life is still laughing at you, behind your back and kicking hell out of your sand castle of plans.

Whatever.

I have Piggles that remind me life is distracting me from them. They need snuggles.

Bun says, I'm going to continue to ignore your ramp. Where's my snap peapod?

The flock reminds me plans are stupid and I should just chill and kiss beaks all day.

So I did. All of that. Because life is short and plans can get in the way of important things like happy.

6-7-17

If you called today gloomy, it would be the right color. But I love dark, rainy days so the connotation would be wrong. The thunder isn't crashing, just a faint but felt rumble from the sky. The rain is consistent and very heavy. I can only see rain curtains through the windows.

Felix is asleep on top of his tent. Kirby is on my shoulder grinding his beak. Butters is on top of the 7 foot tree stand, relaxed and preening. Snickers is watching the rain from the other tree stand. He's busy inspecting his foot.

When the thunder does crash Butters growls disapproval. Bun and piggles are fast napping on top of their personal mounds of hay.

I like this rainy day. I may just curl up on the couch and write in pencil on paper. I just might.

6-8-17

I've recently enrolled myself in Crow University. I'm a freshman. I've been enrolled in the University for the Confused and Ridiculous for over 5 years now. Alas, I continue to flunk out of "Identifying your Confused 101". I'm not sure if I'll ever graduate. The University's Founder, Felix, refuses to grade on a curve.

Thankfully, Jack showed up. Jack and Jill showed up this Spring. I believe they are nesting in the big pine across the field behind our house. I also believe Jack is the son of Edger and Helen Crow. Seeing how they fledged their full nest of babies in our backyard last Spring. And so Jack returns, with his wife. They aren't feeding at the same time, so I'm pretty sure they have eggs on the nest.

The rains came hard this week, and the Blue Jays are still jerks. Jack took matters into his own hands and showed up on our deck furniture 3 days ago rather than waiting on the fence. Calling, flashing, and dancing on the other side of the window he obviously was sending his letter of acceptance to me. So, now I am a freshman in Crow University.

In today's class I learned that Jack will show up at 7:38 am. Jack does not like blueberries. Jack does not like parrot pellets. Jack does not want that thing that is supposed to be interesting called dried banana chip. Jack wants grapes. Jack will accept peanut butter on flax crackers as well. Jack will tolerate nuts.

Yesterday's class I learned Jack now owns our deck. Jack does not care about Butters or Snickers yelling at him. Jack will show up randomly in the afternoon, and thus I must prepare Jack's preferred so that I can answer his call randomly. If Jack is on the left hand green chair, Jack is not interested in food. He is simply owning it like a boss. If Jack is jumping between plastic table chairs calling and flashing his wings; I am taking too long. He'll probably die of the low blood sugars.

I am now convinced Crow University is a subsidiary of the University for the Confused and Ridiculous. Imagine my surprise when I realized Felix was recruiting crows for his World Dominations. I hope Jack grades on a curve.

6-14-17

And so it begins. Nature has her way, and I'm pretty sure all of nature is holding nightly meetings. Mostly just Jack the Crow and Preggers the Squirrel.

I'm minding my own business in the bird room, uncovering the Horde, opening shades, talking to myself, while waking to the day. Up goes the first blinds looking out onto the deck outside. And there on Jack's begging chair, is Preggers the Squirrel, standing up on hind legs, baby belly in resplendent view as evidence for her need for sustenance, STAT. Preggers has adopted the "Jack's in Town, Feed me Seymour, Please, Sir, May I Have Another" stance of panhandling.

She waves her little front paws, blinking away tears of starvation and suffering.

Boy is she pregnant.

An hour later Jack shows up. He's upgraded his Panhandling Technique to landing directly on the table where I lay out the food, jumping up and down crowing, and giving me the Eye of "No, I don't need any food, I want it. Because I'm not stupid like that. What's for breakfast? You're moving slow today lady."

Nature. A kind and gentle breeze in the air reminding us all it doesn't matter who we are, we are all too slow.

6-15-17

LeoBun has toenails like Wolverine. I am really looking forward to seeing Wolverine getting his pedicure at our Vet's today. Simply because I have no idea how one executes a bunny pedicure.

I'm bringing popcorn and a beverage to this show.

6-19-17

My lizard ate my finger. I have no idea if I am nutritious or tasty, but Donotelli took a mealworm size portion of my finger this past Friday. Call me surprised. Call me lunch.

I preach unreasonable expectations all day long about parrots, and then I expect a 7 inch leopard gecko to distinguish between me and his lunch when I'm holding his lunch. I've been handfeeding my leos since they were 1 inch long. Because sMothering companions requires hands on focus in my book. Until it doesn't. Did you know a 7 inch leopard gecko has blazingly sharp needley demon teeth you can't see?

Donotelli is the Ginsu Knife of lizards.

You might be thinking things I don't want to know directly, or you might be thinking "Gosh Kath, what made you think handfeeding toothed lizards was, you know, a good idea?" My rebuttal would simply be, "BECAUSE silly, how do I know they are eating fair amounts of food in the same cage if I'm not the one serving dinner?"

I ordered lizard feeding tongs through my Amazon Prime today. I could use my chop sticks I suppose, but that would be weird.

6-23-17

I learned new things today.

Jamal-Pierre and Werthers went to the vet for wellness checkups and pedicures. I learned they are perfectly perfect.

I also learned they travel well together if I throw a towel over them. Two quiet lumps.

I learned Felix jams hard to Nathanial Rateliff and the Night Sweats. Don't we all Felix?

I learned shopping Friday midday at Publix gets you the good stuff before the crowds descend after 5 pm to get the good stuff. I got some good stuff.

I learned LeoBun has not forgotten about his trip to the vet, and the unmentionable nature of said visit. I can only brush him if I climb into the condo, with a contrite spirit and tone. I still can not be trusted.

I learned the Horde love English Peas. Uncooked. Scattered heavily in their main foraging dish on the aviary floor. There will be English Pea shrapnel on the wall today.

Kirby loves English Peas, too. On the counter, near the grocery bags yet unpacked, so he can crawl in to see what's in the bag, and conveniently crawl out and grab a pea.

I can't say Kirby helps unpack groceries. He's more like a border patrol agent at the crossing between Juarez, Mexico and El Paso, TX. He KNOWS something is up, and is ready to tear everything apart to prove it.

6-28-17

Butters was an absolute drama queen at the vet's today. We know it was all show because her heart rate did not match her mouth rate. At. All.

I learned our little girl is becoming a woman. Eggs may be on the way. Far be it from me to discuss the details of the female ways of creating potential life, but lets just say she's got serious dilation. Like drunk search walking in your house, in the dark, trying to find the bathroom dilation. So dilated.

She's currently clinging to me on my shoulder because that whole vet episode was horrible and terrifying and she almost died. Can you see I'm almost dead? She also smells like sunshine. We sat for a while in dappled shade under our front yard oak tree. I handed her fresh mimosa flowers through her travel cage bars. She just bursts in sunshine smell.

So love this girl. Er...woman.

6-29-17

My daughter gifted me a beautiful set of hand sculpted and painted ceramic lizard and frog statues. These two ceramics sit on the top shelf of my office display shelving, to left of my computer. Right in front of a gorgeous candle holder my husband wood worked for me. Art. I glance at these and think of those I love, and art that inspires my day dreaming. I enjoy this display and I very much enjoy how the lizard and frog sit, the frog is splayed out ready to jump, the lizard is stretched out to rest.

Kirby is currently yelling at the lizard.

He's perched on the top shelf, lightly donking the lizard with his beak once in a while and giving it what for with little screeches and chirps of correction. He is dressing down that lizard with extreme prejudice.

I don't know what that lizard did, but I hope he's learned his lesson.

6-30-17

If I didn't know better I'd say Kirby has a tapeworm.

He is THE food motivated parrot of the house and attacks everything he can get his face into, with great joy and chirpiness.

If I try to scratch my nose he lands on my shoulder like a heat seeking missile. Obviously my hand to face means I'm trying to eat something without letting him know about what I'm trying to eat. I am a traitor. And so is my itchy nose.

I'm in the kitchen chopping vegetables. ZAP! Kirby appears!

I'm filling bowls with fresh morning rations. BAM! Kirby.

Eat an apple. ZIP! Kirby beak suddenly appears between me and my apple. Which was never my apple anyway. Obviously.

Crinkly bags, baggie rustling, Tupperware pop, refrigerator door swish, utensil clinks, microwave door bangs, liquid pours, and scratching my nose makes Kirby Radar detection without fail.

That bird can fly down a stairwell like it's a time continuum wormhole in space. I'm certain he bends time. I can feel it in the air like static electricity.

Or it might be Kirby's happy eating buzzing sound.

7-5-17

You can't legislate intelligence or morality. This is a known. But you can legislate to guide the foolish and immoral down paths to keep those that can guide themselves well, safe.

The Florida State laws ban most, permit a few and only allow a handful of consumer fireworks. Basically you can have poppers and sparklers, and you have to be 16 years or older to use them. The rest need permits, and the most are simply banned.

Banned because it's 2017. Banned like smoking in buildings is banned. Because we now know that smoking will kill you, and others around you. We also know that fireworks are dangerous, filthy, heavy metal carrying, stress inducing, environmental disasters. Those are facts. If you light fireworks you are taking in heavy metals, playing with 1500 degree fire, and menacing your neighbors, local wildlife and leaving a trail of pollution. That's fact. Own that fact if you are going to do it. They were invented to sound and look JUST LIKE WAR.

Make America Great again? Fireworks are made in China. The global capital of environmental disaster and molestation.

But I digress. Consumer Fireworks are illegal in the Great State of Florida. Ironically, you can buy them by signing an affidavit claiming you will only use them for agricultural and hatchery application. So when you purchase illegal contraband and sign that paper, you are also committing fraud. Double ironically because our State Legislators is more worried about the idea that the laws are "forcing parents to lie", not my words, one of the elected hangers on. But let's set aside the pity for the parent with the 4 year old that wants to hold and fire a roman candle.

Let's get down to the nitty gritty. Mayor Rick Kriseman, why are you not enforcing State and County Laws in our beautiful City? Pinellas County Commissioners, why are you not enforcing State and County Laws in the beautiful county of Pinellas? Florida State Governor and Legislation, never mind. You're the ones who set this Ponzi scheme of sales taxes in play. I'll only ask you to sit down and take a nap.

Last night within 100 or less feet of our backyard and home we watched a family gathering of unintelligent and morally challenged individuals commit YouTube quality dumb for 4 hours. 5 year olds running around firing roman candles into trees. Adults grouping multiple bottle rocket tubes, with their T-shirts, and then, with those same 5 year olds huddled around their armament of massively stupid, trying to light all the fuses at the same time. Because gosh, they all have the same label, so their fuses will all burn at the same rate, right?

Their T-shirt Fireworks would fail of course, and the pile of tubes would fall over inevitably sending molten metals skipping across the grass for 30 feet chasing the 5 year olds who are herding and screaming with sparklers.

These redcup adults would then insert fireworks upside down in the launching tubes so that when lit and ignited, the sparkling glowing fire masses would fly out and over into all directions for 50 feet or so and into our yard. In all fairness I can't say if they did this purposefully, or they were just stupid. I honestly do not know.

These redcup adults, (I call them redcup adults, because it seems you have to carry a redcup of adult beverages while lighting fuses with 5 year olds. I think it's their own private special little game.) These redcup adults set massive charges into trees, toward our home and into infinity with grand, stupid, selfish, ignorant style.

I'm not sure what frustrated me more, the endangerment of their little ones, or their stupidity. The level of incompetence and ignorance was historic. Not uncommon on the 4th I suppose, but historic. Legally, all those fireworks were banned, and they should have been stopped, and fined. I suppose it's hard to find these criminals, in as much as they are only sending 100 foot glowing and crashing signals into the sky. I suppose enforcing this law would be down right impossible. At night, in the dark, when the glow of crashing lights are far above trees and roofs pointing the way to their ground zero of stupid.

Just too difficult I suppose.

Wait, what if instead of forcing those poor unfortunate families to commit fraud at time of purchase of these things we make them purchase a permit, paid in full, along with the fireworks. And we charge them an environmental impact fee. Because like smokers, they are impacting every square inch of environment around them.

How about those permits go to local entities who keep them on file. And we spread the word to residential citizens that the law protects their rights, their property and their sanity and they have the right to call police for enforcement of said laws! You know, that old serve and protect thing. When someone's house gets a a roof full of poorly aimed molten fireworks, their homeowner's insurance carrier will have a place to go to get a bit of reimbursement.

How about that?

Or is it all just easier to let military veterans with PTSD and anxiety suck it up. I'm sure they thoroughly enjoy reliving times of violence, rage, death and fear. Let our older citizens turn up their TV and hope it ends soon. It's not like they are doing anything fun anyway. Old people are boring. Let companion animals of all personalities fight through instinctive fear through drugs or other consumer products. They're just animals anyway. The wildlife can go somewhere else for the afternoon and evening. They can suck it up, too. Air, water and soil pollution? Meh. Who cares.

Maybe it's just easier to throw the dice and hope the ER room doesn't get overwhelmed, the children don't get burned and the adults man up. It's only once a year. We are free in this country! We can do what we want.

Oh, but wait.

There are laws already debated and signed ending those thoughts and answering those concerns.

Last night was one of the worst 4th of July's we've dealt with in a long time. Our bird room was filled with sounds of war, lights and flashes and the like. For 4 hours we all just survived an assault. Our next door neighbors jumped in at 10 with the same level of stupid, raining firework shrapnel onto our roof. The local neighborhood sounded like Mosul quietly going into that goodnight. Preparing for the morning's assaults. Snap, pop, BANG. Random. Coming and going and luckily the folks across the street at the lake decided to hold a couple big boomers for midnight. Because it's always great to end on a high, loud, abusive note.

This morning I feel assaulted. (And from a woman who has been literally assaulted, that means something) Our local wildlife must feel the same way, as they didn't show up in our yard for breakfast. Our birds, our flock suffered. Particularly Butters and Snickers. I am more than angry on that mark. I am infuriated. I am infuriated for every human and companion and wild thing that suffered last night.

For what? To celebrate Independence Day. Most don't know the full 5 year history before and after that date (and it wasn't July 4th). Most just want to blow shit up. And some will blow their own hand off, or set their child on fire, or start a wildfire. How about we leave fireworks to the professionals, on sites designated for this environmental impact. How about we remember consumers need labels telling them not to eat detergent pods.

Every single one in the State of Florida is breaking a law that guarantees safety to property and mind. What I want to know, what I want an answer to is this; WHY AREN'T THE LAWS ENFORCED AS WRITTEN!?

Mayor Rick Kriseman? Pinellas County Commission? You're off the hook Governor. I expect just under zero from you and your colleagues in Tallahassee. Although the State Ledge (as the newspapers like to refer to the hangers on with votes and benefits) made these laws and they are supposed to be enforced, actively shared with citizens, and on the books clearly.

WHY AREN'T THE LAWS ENFORCED AS WRITTEN?

7-10-17

Gone for 3 days visiting parents and family up north. Our visit was spectacular and left me coughing for air laughing so hard. I'm pretty sure my parent's neighbors were well aware of my arrival and our gatherings without looking out windows. I'm also pretty sure they were closing windows.

Getting home was spectacular, and fed my soul with that happy you can't quite explain. Kirby was so excited to see me he latched onto my shoulder and repeated in frantic machinegun style, kirbygivemeakissyouragoodboykirby-kissyou'rebeingagoodboykirby!" All the while kissing my cheek and looking into my eyeball. I'm not sure if he found anything behind it.

Snickers, Butters and Felix were all shouting greetings of Hi!, Hello!, and Bye Bye! Because sometimes there aren't enough ways to say hello.

Piggles running up to their cage walls to say hello...or maybe to see if I brought anything good to eat.

It was probably a hello. Nothing to do with food at all.

Bun didn't move from his belly flopped napping position. But he did nod an ear. So I got that going for me.

The Horde chirping greetings and jumping to the front of the cage, I'm sure to welcome me home. That had nothing to do with just wanting to get the door open. I'm certain is was about me and my arrival home.

A warm embrace from my best friend and husband. His family visiting and waiting with him to say hello as well.

You know you're world can't be filled any fuller when, no matter the landing, it's in the middle of an ocean of love.

And yes, I am guilty of saying hello to the flock before my husband. But he gets me. Which is why he's my best friend forever.

7-12-17

Snickers moved the goal posts this morning. He started this yesterday, I suppose he was test driving my ability to catch on. I caught on, and am now required to give wing pit massage, head massage and wing adorations before this chicken will leave the bathroom in the morning.

Basically the new and improved official Snicker Mornings Procedure includes the following; morning carpet bomb in the shower, followed by TwoHandsFull jumping to the counter then up and onto Dad's Cologne and Sundry box on said counter. There he can admire himself in the mirror while looking over his shoulder at me with an urgent whiny growl. It's time for massage. Start at the nairs around the nostrils, move back over the head and neck, under the chin, down the little naked throat path and back again.

Snickers will then open his wings fully and I'm supposed to say, "Pretty wings!" while gently running my hands down the fronts of his shoulder to the tip of the longest flight feathers. "Pretty WINGS!"

I can't forget that part. I was admonished for forgetting that part yesterday.

Snickers closes his wings with a satisfied wing flap and we repeat until Snickers grabs my pointer finger and says, "HUH?"

I'm pretty proud of myself. I got all that straight on the second try. It's like I was born to be trained or something.

7-13-17

Leonidas the Rabbit is a stick shift. I found that out last night. I thought he was an automatic, but nope, he's a stick.

I can put him in neutral with his ears, so I can brush his butt fur. I found that out last night when I was rubbing his ears and brushing him. I slipped him into neutral and brushed all his butt fur right down to his feet. He didn't move an inch. His eyes were closed, and he was parked, engine running.

If you have a bun, I'd double check their transmission.

7-16-17

There was a knock on our door early this morning. I say early because it's Sunday and any knock before, say, 10 am, is early.

I lay in bed hearing that knock and decide to dismiss it as a LeoBun morning call for breakfast, because it's early. And I have not engaged my brain beyond the need to daydream.

Not long after I finally engage enough brain to brush my teeth and navigate a staircase a thought passes. In that moment of stair navigation and thoughts of coffee I think to myself, "I think that was a door knock." I grab my phone. Because only one person knocks on our door early, randomly, always sending a text and leaving a surprise. She's rather like an Easter Bunny with a smart phone. Text, knock, gift. Hop.

I was right on both counts. The knock was hers, and she left a gift at the door as she promised in that text. Tomorrow's my birthday, and my little sister never fails to randomly remind those she loves, that she loves them. She never fails. She is a magical Easter Bunny of love. Quietly. Randomly. And with insightful kindness, she leaves tokens of reminders of love and personal family understanding.

Me, I just sleep in when I can. Older sisters require alot of patience I bet. I should text her and ask.

7-18-17

How to Party like it's 1999 when you turn 54;

I gave yesterday quite a bit of thought the week before. The weekend prior, Cali would remind me it was my weekend and asked if I wanted to do or get or have anything special. He's like that, which is why he's my best friend.

I thought for a moment each time he asked and reminded me of that birthday weekend fact. And every time I looked around in thought I realized I was living inside a life fully lived and I just didn't need or want for anything. Of course, I would have teleported my kids and family in, that goes without saying. But since we talk every day one way or the other, that idea wasn't an ache so much as a thought. I had, after all, just gotten back from my hometown visit for my Father's birthday weekend and spent amazing immersive time with my parents, kids, and family. I am satiated and content.

I arted all weekend. Played with parrots, watched a movie (Okja, on Netflix. Do what you have to to see this movie), and happily went about my 48 hours with my best friend.

By mid Sunday I knew what I was going to do on my Birthday. I had so many wonderful voices, wishes, gifts, hugs, cards and kindness coming in from all directions. I decided to take it all in, mindfully still, on a couch, with parrots watching Minion Movies, and Lego Batman movie.

Because seriously I had no choice. All the parts were available to build this birthday. Cali brought home the Lego Batman Movie for me, Catherine sent me Lego shaped candy (which you can build with while you eat) and our kids sent gorgeous flowers that sat next to me while I texted birthday wishes back and forth, ate Lego candy, and sat on a couch with parrots watching movies that make me laugh.

I did get up between Despicable Me and Despicable Me 2 to pop popcorn and grab a water with a beer. (Duly note, you need to hydrate while you dehydrate. It's a zero sum game that way).

Butters, Snickers, Felix, Kirby and I plowed through popcorn and left the couch looking like a row of seats at a movie theater. The Horde had a bowl of their own in their aviary, in as much as cockatiels are louder than any movie soundtrack.

I got up again between Despicable Me 2 and Minion Movie Shorts to refresh the idea of snacks, water and beer. And brush the popcorn off the couch and onto the floor. We are a civilized crew.

I got up again between Minion Movie Shorts and Lego Batman Movie for refreshing refreshments and brushing the last refreshments off the couch again. Seriously, at this point, what's the point? By this time the Butters, Snickers and Felix are full and all want naps in their cages on their favorite spots. So it's me and Kirby on the couch. Kirby decided he'll nap inside my shirt, laying on my chest. Of course that forced my hand and I could no longer eat snacks like a drunken Viking. I mean, I didn't want to bury the bird in popcorn, almonds and snacks.

After Lego Batman Movie, we all just slid back into some sort of semblance and by the time Cali got home the house was put back together and I was officially 54 (according to the time on my birth certificate).

I do have one question unanswered though. I've asked this question of myself at every birthday. Why am I being celebrated? I floated around for 9 months and took a slip n slide into the world. Honestly, Mom should be the one getting the gifts. I barely did anything at all. Although I probably looked adorable.

I'm pretty sure I did do that, that day.

7-19-17

Seagulls are the unruly 7 year old gangs of the sky. Loud, pushy, impatient, totally oblivious to etiquette and decorum, and loud. A single seagull call is romantic essence left in the air. Half a dozen or better sitting on your fence hollering at your windows in complete disarray and disappointment is Children of the Corn. You get the feeling someone's gotta die.

I fed leftover chopped chicken to a 14 member group of these guys a few days back. And really we have to go back a day for the full picture of the Seagulls of the Corn moment.

One lone romantically essenced seagull showed up during the late afternoon dinner service. We were serving about 30 at that time. Squirrels, doves, crows, blue jays, and about 14 Ibis. A good crowd, generally well behaved and obvious regulars to Cafe de LaFollett. They kept to their favored seats. We are a seat yourself establishment. Very French street cafe. Donc très français.

So this one lone seagull, let's call him Jerry. Jerry shows up. He seems lost, but interested in the menu. I feel for Jerry. He's new here, and the regulars are like the regulars at Katz's Deli. You better know what you want and you better get it, and get seated and out of the way. Or you know, that'll be the last time you try and get in this line.

I like Jerry. I go outside with a container full of chopped rotisserie chicken and chopped rotisserie chicken skin. This is where it gets hairy. Jerry, being a seagull decides he needs to eat and fly at the same time, because...seagull. The Ibis are annoyed, the crows get irritated and instead of taking off, they decide they'll go ahead and join in the feasting of said rotisserie.

I am easily amused.

Duly note; Ibis like teeny tiny chopped chicken. Crow like anything that shows up by their feet. And blue jays are insulted. But a seagull like Jerry. He's all about that roasted skin.

I end the feasting by closing the lid on the container and going back in the house. I giggle for a while and we just smile about our own natural habitat of slightly weird.

Next day Jerry shows up with his gang. I ran out of the chicken, and the chicken skin, and grapes and did my best to make sure the Ibis and crows got a reasonable facsimile of a fair share. Meal service went well all in all, but I did run out of mise, but then again nothing died on the pass and I really only felt I got weeded for about 10 plates anyway.

Yesterday Jerry did a fly over. But he was early. Sorry Jerry. We really don't open until 4. He must have reported back to the gang at the Target parking lot that Cafe de LaFollett isn't serving the special chicken anymore, because the gang hasn't been back.

Which is fine, they were creeping me out and totally throwing off dinner service.

7-20-17

Snickers has been a very methodical molter this year. If he drops/pulls one on the right, he drops/pulls one on the left. Wing, belly, butt or head...it makes no difference. He has become a very symmetrical parrot in 2017. He's also going through an extended heavier molt and seems to be upgrading every square inch of Snickers.

He's currently on my head. He just removed a shorter tail feather, and handed it to me. Which in Snickers speak means donked me in the face with it and dropped it on my keyboard between my typing hands. It's a beautiful feather. But wait, there's one more, but this time he's not offering it to me, this one he needs to be chewed on for a bit.

While hanging it in front of my face.
Laughing.

Snickers, the symmetrical methodical molting clown.

7-24-17

Comforting habits. That's what I call them. Things I do to reassure my brain that I am on the right path, all is well, and I can move on to the next goal. I have to check the stove before bed. Even if we never used it that day. I must lightly touch each dial to make sure it is in the off position. I have to check all the deadbolts visually before bed, too. I need to hear each parrot purr, grux shift on their perch in their bedroom cage before I can sleep. I have to kiss my husband and tell him one last time for the day that I love him. These things happen in a particular order. I leave my husband for last, so you know, he's the last thing on my mind.

I know I'm not the only one, but rather one of a million. I also know rarely does anyone question or try to explain another's need for comforting habits. We except them as a normal human condition. The healthy kind is, the kind that releases a mind, rather than entrap it in repetition.

Snickers morning massage moment is now a comforting habit. He needs it to move on with his day. Kirby needs a big good morning, and then time to throw all the food he personally doesn't like out of every one else's food bowls. The Horde require baby talk, clean water, a move to their favorite window and fresh greens on top of their foraging bowl. Then more baby talk.

Butters requires three "Huh?", one "SNICKERS!" and me responding, "Butters! You are my silly Butter Bean, let's go!" while sitting on top of the bedroom door.

The key to all this is Butters pooping on the back of the door while I'm in the middle of the Snickers Morning Massage Moment while Kirby is flying up and down the stairs goading me to get on with it so I can watch him throw everyone's food out while Felix is on his tent by my computer shouting, "HERE!" because I'm not there, and the Horde chirping at newly discovered decibel levels trying to get Kirby's attention.

It's all VERY technical really.

7-27-17

Kirby is turning into a latching lurker. Like a jet fighter, landing on a aircraft carrier. He comes flying around a corner, all I hear are engines, and then he latches onto my shirt, dumps the engines, leaving his little claws and my shirt as the only things keeping him from from the abyss in front of us.

He came in so fast and furious yesterday he almost overshot the shoulder runway and ended up hanging upside down by one claw and looking up at me from my chest.

"Weeehwww!" Was the pilot's only comment.

8-3-17

Louie and Benny, inseparable sons of Winston and Stella. Independent of everything but each other to the point of panic. I like to think of these two as the boys to watch. Except for a few white spots on the back of Louie's neck, the two are identical. Oh, and Benny's missing toe. That's a differential.

Felix allows them in his tent.

Kirby follows them around the house. I haven't decided if Kirby is keeping an eye on them in a paternal manner, or if he's making sure these two don't touch anything that belongs to him. I think it's the former though. Generally Louie calls out to Kirby to catch up.

Snickers and Butters seem to view them as mosquitoes.

End of day they are still the sons of Winston and Stella. Winston herds them back to the aviary at 8:30. And because you can't trust them, Winston stations himself in the tree in front of the aviary to stop any last minute flights. Stella cut apron strings long ago.

If you're lucky, and you sit still long enough these two will land on you and travel the easy routes to play with your hair or you clothing. They talk to each other in small chirpas, and travel quickly always on the look out for a reason to explode into flight. If you are really lucky, Louie will give you a kiss before taking off.

They do not step up. I've never bothered to require it of them. They are 100% parrot parent raised with no interference from the human in the room. And yet, they learned about shoulders, heads, hair and dining with humans. And they do all that very well. They just do it all on their time. Which turned out to be flock time.

8-7-17

Living across the street from a lake, and at the end of a tidal creek makes our yard and fence landing zones for all our area's birds; predatory, song, water and whatnot. I consider marsh hens a whatnot. I love the marsh hen's laugh in the middle of the night.

I also love Cornelius. He showed up one day, alone, and fearless. I love this duck. Cornelius always brings news of his day, endlessly talking. He won't fly over our fence. But has no problem sticking his head through it if I'm offering grapes too slowly. I'm going to open the fence gate and invite him in today I think.

Cornelius is a talker. Endless peeps in all variety of ways. He loves Grape Nuts. He gets so excited eating those he gets to peeping so loud and fast he jumps right out of his flat footed flippers. Cornelius has a mohawk. The black line of head feathers raise straight up when he's happy and excited and telling me stories.

I just love this duck.

With every visit he's more talkative. He's learning the ropes, and has no problem waiting for a squirrel to get out of his way. He comes in from the South, and leaves the same way. Pausing on our neighbors fence to preen one last time before flying off.

I feel like a duck drive thru fast through restaurant. He flys in, parks by our fence, tells me things, I fill his order and we visit. He talks the entire time he eats. Then he does the most elaborate preening style. Pulling oil off his oil gland with his chin, and working that over his body. His first two flight feathers are white. Bright white. He is amazing. He is fearless. He brought a friend.

She was a big brown hen of a Muscovy, and she was not impressed with anything I offered or any part of me. I'm pretty sure I received the Eye of Disdain off that girl.

Cornelius was impressed though and we visited as his friend waddled off indignant at the idea of grubbing off a human.

I love this duck.

8-8-17

Our nightly routine includes emptying leftover parrot bowl foods into the backyard area for the local wildlife. We're a drive-in food pantry. Every one starts lining up about 5-ish EST.

Squirrels, doves, blue jays, the cardinal couple from the tree next door, crows, ibis, mockingbirds, and a random egret. They start assembling on, and on the other side of, our chain link fence knowing I'll be showing up with bowls to empty and towels to shake out.

I walked out onto our patio to head to the fence line, arms full of the evenings menu items, and there's Cornelius, half way between me and the fence. Happy face, wings flapping, and ready for dinner. He ran straight for me with wings open and peeping loudly. Obviously, he was starving like a guinea pig left alone for 30 minutes. I had to sideline the food pantry of course. Cornelius has stolen my heart and my attention span. I set towels and bowls on the patio table and ran back into the house to get his favorites.

We sat in the grass together, Cornelius and I, while he impatiently ate crushed grapes and apple bits. He talked with his mouth full, wildly telling me about something somewhere, that was some thing amazing. At least that's the gist of it I think.

He ran out of his portion and looked at the bag of grapes that sat next to my lap long enough to explain his intent. Which was basically attacking the bag and trying to eat more grapes through that bag. Three good hard attempts left him peeping at me as if this whole problem was my fault. It was, so I fixed it by crushing 5 more grapes and hand feeding Cornelius.

He peeped loud in one satisfied expression announcing his satiation. And turned around and started walking to the main double door gate at the front of the house. It's got a 1 foot clearance from the ground. I watched the duck saunter from our dinner spot, lower his head and disappear on the other side.

Because Cornelius is a complete distraction for me I had to sneak a peak through the wood slats to see what he was up to.

He found a good spot in the sun, on our driveway, and was preening proudly. He was there when Cali got home from work. The big red Tundra meant not a thing to Cornelius. He watched Cali park, and then sauntered off into the grassy area of the lawn next to the driveway and foraged more.

I. Love. This. Duck.

8-10-17

Yesterday afternoon Cornelia stepped up on our deck to put a rush order on her meal.

I need to stop here and update a few matters. Cornelius is a Cornelia. I appreciate the help in the matter of gender with this duck. I also appreciated very much the video collection given to me to listen to the two genders speak. It's pretty clear who is who once you hear a duck speak. So...Cornelia. She's a she and not a he and still my distraction and my obsession.

Back to the deck scene yesterday. She was a few feet from the deck, looking at the door when we caught sight of her. And you know there's something magical about catching the eye of a duck. We saw each other through the window glass and ran to meet. Rather like one of those slow motion romance movie scenes. Except I'm not a duck.

Anyway. She came 3 feet onto the deck and paused looking around and feeling the enclosure of it. She stopped and walked backwards matching me step for step. Her chosen distance; a couple feet. So I sat on the edge of the deck and Cali and I both fed Cornelia, taking turns. We chatted again about her day. Cali saying I needed to offer more than grapes for her. Me, in agreement. She ate well, bid her goodbyes and that was that.

This morning she was waiting in the shade just off the deck, in the grass, on the east side. I was in the process of setting up shop for parrots, bun and piggles. But brake-check!

I ran out to meet her with a few blueberries, grape nut cereal, grapes and a piece of cantaloupe. She ate out of my hand. I'd like to think it was because she wanted the physical contact. Most likely it was being inpatient for breakfast. But, no matter.

She ate well, bid her good morning and headed out to her day, and I back into mine.

As I was doling out fresh hay to the piggles and LeoBun this morning I realized I am just one goat away from farm status.

I really hope a goat shows up today.

8-14-17

Cornelia showed up at high noon today. Normally she's an early morning, late afternoon girl. I saw her fly in and land on the opposite side of our fence. She just meandered around for a minute or two and starting walking our fence line.

I ran out with her bag of grapes to say hello. She's hilarious. We've got an eroded spot under the fence in one place. She heard me unlock the door and barreled straight for that sweet spot under the fence. It's a Cornelia sized tunnel. We met at the deck and I sat down while she ate from my hand for a few grapes. She wasn't hungry really.

My girl just came for a visit. She walked down to the corner of the deck and hopped up, then walked back to my spot and literally sat down two duck lengths away from me.

There we were looking out over the open field. She peeped a while and preened, working her oil through her feathers.

I just watched her and smiled.

Snickers, Butters and Kirby were in the windows giving me the Eye of SERIOUSLY!?!?!

Three parrots with six parrot eyes stared out the window.

Cornelia said her goodbyes by pooping on the deck. Which in my world is a favorable response.

We should build a mini duck pond...with a meandering mini creek...that meanders under the deck, around the crepe myrtle and turns into a mini waterfall to fill the mini duck pond. I think this would be really great for Cornelia.

I. Love. This. Duck.

8-15-17

I've been working with the piggles at night, during evening dinner service. No one gets a carrot without a nose boop. I gotta get paid. Now they come running up the side of their condo, tippy-toed and jumpy, noses straight in the air. BOOP! And a carrot. I am a carrot vending machine.

Butters digs being on my shoulder while I play guitar. She's really good about the requirements. Shoulder rider must face forward. (Parrot poop on a guitar...total party foul) Shoulder rider must not chew on guitar strap. Shoulder rider must not pull glasses off head of shoulder owner. Shoulder rider can sing, but not directly into shoulder owner's ear hole. No eating while shoulder riding. I have to give her credit, she's graduated with full honors. Snickers is a drop out.

Yesterday I took a suggestion of a good friend and added a fresh water bowl to Cornelia's visit. Now I really didn't see how this was going to be interesting to her. We live on that tidal creek, and the lake is right across the street. I rather felt I was being redundant. So I thought I'd upgrade this bowl idea by adding grapes and blueberries to the water. Cornelia loves bobbing for fruit. Loves as in gets so excited she peeps and almost quacks. She loves this so much she ran off Preggers the squirrel who came over to see what the commotion was about. She loves this so much that when she runs out of fruit to bob for, she will run over to me and order more fruit and run back to the bowl and wait with the Eye of HURRY UP! I need a wet bar and mini fridge on the deck.

8-15-17

Cornelia and I have a system worked out. In the morning she stands on the deck, at the edge, staring straight through the door window. A peeping Cornelia if you will. I wave hi, she jumps off the deck and waits at the edge with wing flaps and peeps.

In the early evening I pace between the door window and two windows on either side of that door looking for Cornelia. A reverse peeping mom if you will. She walks into view, I jump and run outside with her bowl of water and favorites.

We are a balanced codependent couple.

Felix flew today. He decided Snickers, Butters and I were taking far too much time with the morning wake up call upstairs. He landed on the 10th stair, with 3 to climb up to get to the master bedroom. After his epic landing he called out, "See the birdie?"

"Not yet Felix." I was just being honest.

After one step successfully climbed, "See the birdie?"

"Keep climbing Fee!" A mom should be supportive and helpful.

Step two, mounted. "See the birdie?"

"No, but I hear a birdie!" A mom stating the obvious. I am so confused.

He scrambled up to the second floor and with slow methodical grey footsteps he walked into the master and announces, "Hey! See the birdie?"

Snickers scrambled up onto his roost cage, looked down at Felix and yelled, "HUH? STOP!"

Now we are downstairs and Felix is up on top of the master bathroom door whistling with grand satisfaction. I'll need to get a Snickers off my head and go back up there and get Felix, once he's done fart sound singing. He's currently laying down some beats. Far be it from me to interrupt his jam session.

8-16-17

My nest here is full and busy and happy. This is my second nesting really. We have a son and daughter who left to find their own places to nest. You think my duck is awesome? You should meet our daughter. She's hilarious, intelligent, strong and true. Driven to never give up and when life puts her feet to it, she'll burn a bridge and pave a road at the same time.

I think on her in her nest with a man she loves and who loves her back with fierce loyalty and necessary humor. She is blazing her trail to a success she has worked on for years now. I think on her today, about to step out into a new experience to build on that trail. Most likely she's terrified with a gooey center of excited. She'll own today, because that is what she does.

I am in awe of her.

You should meet our son. He's traveled a long road in his own head. Too many obstacles were put there by others with less honor. We talked today. He has started on a journey that took some intestinal fortitude, deep breathes and a bit of "screw it, I'm gonna do it" on the side. I think on him today. Searching the corners of his reality and deciding he will be who he decides to be with purpose and honesty. What else can a human do really? Honesty with purpose. His inner core has always been a brutal loyalty to honorable things. We say he is an ancient soul in a young man's body. I can feel the wind righting his sails now. I can hear the keel of his life holding true for him. I am in awe of his strength to take one more step forward. Because that's what he does. Even when he hates that step because he is unsure of it. But that was then, this is different.

I am in awe of him.

I am married to a man that can find the humor is the oddest things I cook up. And before I can gather the necessary elements to start this oddly stew, he comes home with bags full of necessary ingredients. He is my very best friend and my soul mate.

I am in awe of him.

I offer my musings because I feel better hidden behind words. It feels safer to show you how I feel about things rather than video or photos directly. This is who I am.

Things in this world are overstimulated, on fire, raging, simmering full and dare I say agitating.

No matter the external rages we read or see, the cure to any and all disruption, hate, and fear (and it is fear that rages most right now) lives inside our homes first. Gratitude, humility, appreciation, and whenever possible, a kinder thought than yesterday.

If we want anything to get fixed, we have to start in the mirror and work our way out from there.

I am overwhelmed every day for those that write me kind words of encouragement and personal stories of their own. I am right now, barely able to vacuum because I have a photo of my daughter taken today as she starts out on another challenge, she's wearing that big smile of hers. I can't really think on dusting. My son and I are discussing living life better and kinder for ourselves and others. And I'm going to crochet him a blanket in his favorite colors because that falls inside that category. My very best friend will be home in a few hours and the flock will rejoice to rattle the rafters, and I will place a kiss on a face that stopped me in my tracks years ago, and still makes my knees a little wobbly.

Today is a glorious, beautiful love filled day. Not because someone told me it was, not because there is no evil in this world. But because I chose to fill my heart and mind with such things.

And yes, I'll finish the vacuuming...this house if filled with Snickers trademark Snickers' Floofy Snow. He just can't molt, he explodes in teeny tiny bits of white stuff that hangs in the air. Which if you catch it in a ray of sunshine is pretty epic in and of itself. I may or may not dust.

I kinda wanna start crocheting.

You'll find the latest musings on my personal Facebook page:
@KathyLaFollett

If you are a parrot person like me and haven't heard of my website or Facebook page I invite you to pay me a visit!

www.flockcall.com
@FlockCall

If you too, are in need of training visit Felix's Facebook page.
Training humans since 2012
@FelixLaFollett

Thank you for sharing my world.

Made in the USA
Columbia, SC
24 September 2020